£3,—

# *Gillian:*
## *A Second Chance*

***Veronica Staunton***

**BLACKWATER PRESS**

Printed in Ireland at the press of the publishers 1991


8 Airton Road,
Tallaght,
Dublin 24.

ISBN 0 86121 323 8

*Editor*
Anna O'Donovan

*Design & layout*
Paula Byrne

# *Contents*

# *Foreword*

On 13th June 1990 our young ten year old daughter Gillian became the Republic of Ireland's first cystic fibrosis sufferer to receive a life saving heart and lung transplant. It was carried out in Great Ormond Street's Children's Hospital in London.

This book is Veronica's account of Gillian's difficult life since she was diagnosed with the fatal disease in 1982.

It was Veronica's great love for Gillian which stimulated her to pioneer such transplants for young cystics. She was not offered a transplant and initiated the whole thing herself in 1987 because she refused to accept that Gillian had to die.

I didn't even believe at that time it was possible to survive with someone else's organs. To me transplantation was another world into which I didn't ever expect to enter. Veronica believed she could overcome all the difficulties, and she did. The problems were enormous but after five assessments in three British Hospitals over a period of three years, it finally happened.

Gillian now enjoys a quality of life she never ever thought possible for herself. It is an interesting human story of our family's survival in very difficult circumstances over a long period of time. I hope the book will give hope to other young cystics or to anyone enduring serious illness. It should give them the courage never to give up and continue the daily battle for their survival. Gillian's own courage, determination, love of life and sense of humour should be a source of inspiration to everyone.

*Brendan Staunton July 1991*

## Dedication

I dedicate this book to my friend Una who has been a true friend in every sense of the word over the past eight years. She is a very fine person who cared.

# 1. Diagnosis

I tightened my grip on the baby sitting on my knee, and did not dare look at Brendan as the young house doctor sitting across the table said, "I'm afraid Gillian's sweat test is highly suggestive of CYSTIC FIBROSIS."

She knew, by the look of horror on our faces, we knew it was fatal.

"You mean Gillian is going to die?" I responded, tightening my two arms even more closely around her waist.

Sensing the tension Gillian wriggled free from my arms and twisting her body, turned around, stood up on my knees and threw her arms around my neck. It was almost as if our beautiful little girl knew we were discussing her lost future. In one minute and one sentence the doctor had doomed Gillian to die and had taken away our hopes and dreams, aspirations and expectations of a long and happy life for our baby.

"Well, Gillian seems to have done very well so far and she is still thriving. The treatment for this disease has greatly improved in recent years," the doctor continued.

"Yes, but it is a killer disease and there is no cure, isn't that correct?"

"Yes, that's right, I'm sorry," she responded.

Gillian started kissing my face and as I looked at her chubby cheeks and beautiful brown eyes I found it difficult to comprehend what we had just been told. Brendan remained absolutely silent. He uttered not so much as one word. He just stared at the doctor as if to say tell me you don't mean all of this.

"Could there be a mistake?" I asked.

"I don't think so, but we are going to re-do the test later today. We will keep her in hospital for a few weeks to clear up the current chest infection."

So much was happening so quickly, and I began to have a physical reaction. My tummy started to turn over and I felt sick. I thought I would vomit. The next statement from the doctor was the final straw to complete the nightmare. "We would like you to bring your other daughter, Kelli-Ann, in tomorrow to have a sweat test to make sure she is clear."

Kelli and Brendan were like two peas in a pod. They looked alike, shared the same temperament, vision of life and musical talent. He stood up, groped his way towards the door and quietly left the room.

I tried to concentrate on what the doctor was saying and cuddle Gillian at the same time. She told me it was a disease which affected multiple organs in the body. The lungs and digestive system were the main organs affected. It is progressive, and because the body produces an abnormal amount of thick mucus, it obstructs the airflow in the lungs and clogs the pancreas. Because of this defect the lungs are prone to infection, therefore, the most important part of Gillian's treatment would be physiotherapy, three times a day, to keep the mucus moved and prevent infection. This treatment, hopefully, would help slow down its progression. We would be taught how to do the physiotherapy. The prognosis would depend on the number of chest infections and the response to treatment. Gillian had been affected in the respiratory system since three weeks of age and already had many chest infections!

Our fears that there was something seriously wrong with Gillian had finally been confirmed. We had been quietly very worried about the baby for quite a while. In our worst nightmare we could never have imagined the devastation of that interview with the young doctor, whose name I don't remember today, eight years later. So, on Wednesday 16th June 1982 we received the awful news that our little girl, just past her second birthday, could die at any time in the near future. This was to be the date we will never forget as long as we live, the day the whole course of our lives was to change. It would never again be the same. A normal life as other people understand it was gone forever.

I think the consultant who had carried out the various tests the previous week had already a good idea of the diagnosis. He had come up to see us when the tests were completed. He would be on holiday, he said, but if we came back the following Wednesday the house doctor would give us the results and he would see us when he returned. We should have known it was going to be on-going, but chose to ignore the implications of his remarks. When I asked him if he thought it was serious, he just said he would prefer not to comment until all the test results were complete.

We had returned home that day the previous week and, quite out of character, we had not discussed Gillian's condition at all during the week we were waiting for the results. She continued to cough constantly, especially at night. We were already getting used to the constant coughing, even before she was diagnosed. The child had been coughing on and off for two years. I used to say to a friend at work, "Joan, she was coughing again last night, I wonder is it anything serious?" I was looking for reassurance that many babies coughed constantly. I kept thinking of the doctor in Portugal, who said, "She will grow out of it!" She didn't, and she wouldn't!

Finally, the interview ended and we were reunited with Brendan in the corridor, and proceeded upstairs to be introduced to the Medical Ward of Harcourt Street Children's Hospital, Dublin, which, in time, was to become Gillian's second home. Half way up the first flight of stairs we passed a big black and white panda in a glass case. My stomach was turning over the first time I set eyes on the panda. From that day, over eight long years ago, to this day, my stomach still turns whenever I set eyes on him. Believe me, I have looked at him hundreds of times since that fateful day. He got dustier, and I older and more worn out each time we met.

Once up in the ward, the routine we were to become very familiar with began – weighing Gillian, charting her height and weight and other information. She weighed two and a half stone or 16 kilos that day. Two years later, at four years of age, she weighed two stone two pounds or 13 kilos. This is what the killer disease, cystic fibrosis, was destined to do to our beautiful baby girl. To look at Gillian that day, no-one would have believed there was anything seriously wrong with her. She looked really beautiful. Her dark hair, beautiful large brown eyes, lovely clear skin and chubby cheeks showed nothing to betray the destruction of her lung tissue which had already begun.

Gillian was a very good baby, as quiet as a little mouse. She only made noise when she was coughing. The smile never left her face and she was at her happiest when she snuggled up to me for a cuddle. Her words were few, and I presumed she was late speaking because she had spent the first year of her life in Portugal and hence, had not been exposed to enough English.

We were asked if we would like to see the social worker and Brendan said, "No thank you, we don't want to speak to anyone".

A young nurse commented that many children with cystic fibrosis now live to about fourteen years. This was supposed to be a consoling comment. She meant, of course, we probably had nothing to worry about in the immediate future. To me, the thoughts of living with and watching a child grow and develop and exchange love for fourteen years and then to lose the child seemed completely soul destroying. It didn't bear thinking about.

No-one knew what to say to us. There was nothing to be said. We were heart-broken, and no words were going to change that.

We had been in the hospital for five hours and already I felt we had left home a month. Gillian sat on my knee, clad in the hospital pyjamas, and was quite happy to observe her new surroundings. It was not until we tried to place her in the cot that she reacted. When she realised it was different than the previous week and she wasn't coming home with us, she screamed the place down and tried to climb out over the top of the cot. I kept telling her we would be back in a while. As we walked down the stairs we could hear her screaming, I wanted to scream myself. It was the saddest day of our lives and we could not believe what had happened to us in a few short hours. It's always other people dreadful things happen to, one never thinks it will come to one's own door.

We stopped briefly in the Montrose Hotel where we had a snack and Brendan drowned his sorrows with a double whiskey.

It was a beautiful sunny evening as we approached the Bowling Club in Bray. Kelli was running around, playing with children, as my parents bowled. One look at our faces and my mother and father knew there was a problem. As my mother walked across the green towards me she said, "Where is Gillian?"

"She's in hospital and she has cystic fibrosis," I blurted out.

I felt as if I were watching someone else say these words. My parents were well aware of what cystic fibrosis was, as my cousin had a little boy with it. My mother had heard from her sister how dreadful a disease it was and about the terrible daily banging of the lungs, to give the child a few years of life.

"I always knew that dreadful cough wasn't normal. I knew it was serious," replied my mother, while my father just stood there with tears rolling down the side of his face.

We all left the green and went back to their house nearby. We had a cup of tea and I asked my mother to feed Kelli and keep her until we came back later that night.

"Will you have to bang the back of that little child every day now, like Bernie has to do to Barrett?" she asked.

"Yes, I'm afraid so."

"Did they give you any idea how long she might live?"
"No, Mum, they don't know".
"Sure, please God, they might find a cure for that disease soon".
"Maybe, but it's difficult to cure anything genetic. Anyway we must go back to her, see you later."
When we arrived at the hospital, Gillian was sitting quietly in the middle of the cot with just pyjama bottoms on and a drip on her arm. She looked at us and pointed to the needle in her little wrist and said. "Sore, there Daddy." She jumped up and held her arms out for Brendan to pick her up. We stayed with her for a couple of hours and then went through the same ritual as when we left her earlier in the day. This time the screams were louder. We could still hear her three flights down in the lobby, because it was late at night and her screams echoed through the silence.
The porter commented, "Someone has a good pair of lungs." If only he had known!
By the time we picked Kelli up and took her home to bed that night, we were absolutely exhausted, mentally, physically and emotionally. This was a state we would be in, on and off, for many years to come. The thought of going through a sweat test with Kelli the next day just overwhelmed us. It just did not seem possible our life could have changed so drastically in a space of twenty four hours. As we fell asleep Brendan's last comment of the day was "If Kelli has it as well, I'll just give up."
Early the next morning I phoned the school and for the second time in twenty-four hours I said, "My baby has cystic fibrosis and my other child is being tested today. I won't be able to work until Monday."
Cystic fibrosis, the words were already becoming familiar to my lips. This was Thursday and the state I was in I wondered how I would teach a class on the Monday!

It was another fine sunny summer day as we set off on the half hour journey to the hospital with Kelli. She kept asking why did we leave her baby sister in hospital. I sat with Kelli for half an hour while she endured the sweat test. In those far off days the antiquated method of extracting sweat didn't agree with our very active five year old. She objected to a container being strapped around her waist and lots of clothes put on, in an already hot room, to extract sweat. She kept trying to pull off the extra clothes and complaining, in complete contrast to Gillian, who the previous week just sat passively without a word while this procedure was carried out.

Kelli kept saying,"Mummy, I'm hot, I'm thirsty, I don't like it here. Where's Gillian? What's wrong?" Poor Kelli, this was the beginning of her getting less attention from us than she needed or deserved, through no-one's fault, just circumstances. Kelli did not understand how different the course of our lives was to become compared to other families. We thought we had a chesty baby and Gillian would grow out of it as she got older and the sleepless nights we all endured would end at some stage. If only we could have seen into the future. On the other hand, if any of us could see into the future, would we have the courage to survive the present?

The physiotherapist came to see us that afternoon. We watched her do the physiotherapy on Gillian. She turned Gillian upside down over three folded pillows and with hands cupped began pounding vigorously on her back. We watched in a daze not believing what was happening. I think Brendan was about to tell her to stop but then we realised Gillian was not crying. She pounded away for a few minutes and suddenly Gillian went into an awful coughing fit. I could see green phlegm oozing out of the side of her mouth. I pulled a tissue out of my bag, Diana the therapist sat her up and she coughed up a substantial amount of green phlegm into my tissue.

"Great, now she will feel better, the IV antibiotics are working already. Normally at this age they just swallow it, she is a bright little thing and very good," said Diana.

Diana was a pleasant looking woman with short grey curly hair. She was very calm and cool and acted as if pounding away on a child's back was quite normal. She then turned Gillian on her right side over the pillows and pounded away again. Next, the same on the left side and after that she sat her up on her knee and pounded the front of her chest. We could see clearly what she was doing. She had cleared four different sections of Gillian's lungs. A container of dirty green phlegm sat on the locker, Gillian smiled and could now breathe more easily. Already we could see the benefit of the physiotherapy. We realised that day that Gillian was quite ill and wouldn't have lasted long if that phlegm was allowed to remain building up on her lungs. Even Diana seemed surprised how productive she was. So, Gillian was to have this treatment three times every day for as long as she lived. Diana explained that when she had an active infection the phlegm would be green, and when she didn't, it would be a white mucus.

We were busy assimilating hospital life and Gillian's treatment during those first few days. We spent endless hours just hanging around the Medical Ward listening to other sick children crying constantly or just making lots of noise playing with toys. We listened to other parents complaining about minor problems and the fact that they had to spend a few days in a hospital. The difficulty for us was the fact that our baby would not get better. We were in a no-win situation and had to accept the fact we could possibly spend a lot of time in this hospital in the future, if we were lucky enough to continue having Gillian. We were embarking on a difficult lifestyle whatever happened and at the end of the road there was only disaster staring us in the face. The whole situation and turn of events overwhelmed us and left us in a state of shock. It was all too much to accept and comprehend. We felt like this without knowing the true reality of what was to face us. Isn't it just as well we sometimes only learn our fate by degrees? I was afraid to let go and cry, although heart-broken, because I felt if I started to cry I would never stop and would just crack up and not be able to go on. Brendan and myself were not at the stage yet where we could verbalise anything. We went through the motions of living those first few days as if in an awful nightmare where we kept thinking we would awake and find out it wasn't real. It never happened.

At twelve mid-day on the Saturday, the phone in the Medical Ward rang and a nurse told me the doctor would like to speak to me. I froze, as we were expecting Kelli's sweat test results. Trembling I picked up the phone. "Mrs. Staunton, Kelli's sweat test is negative, she is clear of cystic fibrosis." Me, being me, I wanted to get into it in more detail and I asked the numerical result and what the normal range was. She told me Kelli's test was 49. The normal range is 0-50, doubtful 50-80 and over 80 positive. When I asked what Gillian's had been she said, "130." But she said this was no indication of how severely affected she was.

I was delighted Kelli was negative but would have preferred her to be more than one point away from doubtful! Brendan smiled for the first time that week and said he was relieved. Negative was negative and he didn't want to go into it any further. I knew he had been very worried that both his children had this killer disease. I really don't know how we would have reacted had we been told they both had it. We almost forgot we had Kelli that week we saw so little of her. She spent most of her time with my parents. It had been the saddest and most traumatic week of my life.

Brendan had lost his mother when he was twelve years of age, so he had already loved and lost, but he said that didn't make it any easier. In fact, he said he already knew how it felt to lose someone close and he understood the implications of the news we had received. On the Sunday night, having left our baby alone in the hospital for the fifth night, it all became too much. I was supposed to be going into a school to teach a class of children the next day. I just didn't feel I could do it. Nothing made sense any more. For the first time in my life I couldn't see any joy, only dark clouds. I told Brendan I just could not face a class ever again, let alone the next day. The only thing I could think about was the fact that I was going to lose my beautiful baby and nothing else had any meaning any more. Brendan understood how I felt but he knew I would have to change my thinking around.

He said, "Look Ron, we haven't lost her yet and things are happening in the medical world every day. We have Kelli, Gillian and ourselves to think about. Why don't you pull yourself together and go back to work, you only have ten days left until your holidays. The school is down the road from the hospital, it will take your mind off it all. We'll see over the summer what we will do for the long term. Let's take each day and do our best. We will fight it together."

It was good advice and I took it. From that day on, I had no choice but to become two people. What I thought and felt was one thing and what I presented to my colleagues and the world was something else.

The next morning, Monday 21st June 1982, Brendan and myself went back to work, Kelli went to school and Gillian continued to adjust to hospital life. It was the beginning of a new life of survival. I fought that first day as I have never fought in my life. I stood in front of a class of teenage children and did a day's work. As I spoke to the children a picture of Gillian kept flashing in front of my face. All I could see was a drip in her little arm and the words cystic fibrosis ringing in my ear. I had made the mistake of calling into the hospital at 8 a.m. to spend a few minutes with her before school. She couldn't understand why I was leaving so soon and kept saying, " No, no, no Mummy, don't go."

I somehow managed to keep my emotions under control that first day. Each day after that it became easier and, in fact, I learned that teaching was helping me, at least for those five hours every day I was not submerged in personal problems and it helped me to forget my reality. It was also a worthwhile job which I was good at and normally enjoyed very much. People were already asking if I was going to give up work and stay at home and look after Gillian. I didn't know!

During those days of Gillian's first hospitalisation I spent all my waking hours with her apart from the five hours a day I was teaching. Every morning before school I went in to get a glimpse of her and came back straight after school. I would drive out to Bray for dinner and then Brendan and myself would drop Kelli at my parents' house and we would head off into Dublin to spend another few hours with her. Brendan was working in Bray from his Hair Studio so he was there for Kelli. I saw very little of poor Kelli during those first few weeks. On the Mondays when Brendan didn't work he would spend the day in the hospital with Gillian. My parents were very good and went in to see Gillian during the early part of the day several times each week.

Gillian responded to the intravenous drugs and the physiotherapy and within a week she was coughing less, eating more and generally looking much better. She would sit on my knee for hours and would never ask to move. As long as she was with me or Brendan she was happy. The coughing stopped completely and it was really difficult to believe she wouldn't come home from hospital and things wouldn't return to their previous state.

Hospital life is another world, as we were quickly learning. We were to experience things we would normally never have come across. Being very caught up in our own problem we couldn't imagine anyone going through worse than ourselves. However, we were touched by another family's plight. One evening about ten days after Gillian was diagnosed a beautiful young girl of around eight years of age with lovely long blond hair lay motionless in a bed. She was close to death. Her father, a tall, well-built man in his thirties hung over her lifeless frame sobbing. The young girl was a victim of leukaemia. We had never seen anything like this before. It seemed so unnatural for the little girl's life to be snuffed out so early. Would we have been affected so deeply by this father's plight had our own circumstances been different?

*Gillian (9 months)*

# 2. Accepting the Reality

So here we were faced with the reality that Gillian had an incurable disease, which affected her digestive and respiratory system. The disease was passed on to her because Brendan and myself possessed the carrier gene within us. Although we were both healthy, there would be a 25% risk of each child we had inheriting the defective gene, and hence having cystic fibrosis. This is exactly what had happened to Gillian. In a case where only one gene is passed from one parent, the person would be healthy but a carrier. If the person misses the gene completely, he or she would carry no risk of passing the disease to future generations. In this part of the world, one in twenty in the general population carries the gene. One in 500 couples are both carriers and one in 2000 babies are born with cystic fibrosis. As far as I know, there are about 800 cystic fibrosis sufferers in Ireland and around 5000 in the United Kingdom.

We had somehow survived the shock of the diagnosis and the trauma of the first two weeks of our new life. I embarked on my summer holidays with relief. There would be nine weeks to relax with Brendan and the children and make a few decisions. Some of the staff were going out for lunch when we finished school for the summer. I couldn't join them because I was collecting Gillian from the hospital, to take her home. Taking the stairs two at a time past the black and white panda, I arrived in the Medical Ward breathless. There she was, already dressed in little blue jeans, red jumper and red sandals, hair shining, with a huge smile and ready to go home. Picking her up I swung her around and said, "How's my baby girl?"

We said our goodbyes hoping it would be a while before we would return. Our lives had been revolving around work and the hospital. I was still in a daze, and the effort of pretending I was alright, in school and around the hospital, was already taking its toll. However, I was to become expert at this pretence in the years to come. My heart was broken in pieces and yet I was saying things like, "Oh well, there are always people worse off."

Brendan and myself had been so busy surviving each day, we had been too exhausted for any discussions. With the advent of the holidays we could relax and talk and console each other. I could stay indoors and really digest this whole thing, on my own, without having to see anyone on a daily basis if I didn't want to. It was lovely to have Gillian home again. In a way, a weight was lifted, because now after almost two years of doubt and niggling feelings and wondering, we at last knew what we had to deal with or at least thought we did. So, it was cystic fibrosis, it had been identified and was being treated. The disease which had crossed my mind often had been leukaemia. I don't know why that particular disease was on my mind, or why I thought it was worse than cystic fibrosis, a case of six of one and half a dozen of the other.

Kelli was delighted to have her little sister home and the hope of seeing more of her Mum. We were a family again, and it was nice. Gillian looked around the bedroom she shared with Kelli, and as she went down to sleep her eyes wandered with interest to the colourful figures of "Popeye and Olive Oil" spread all around the walls. Later that night as the two children slept soundly, Brendan and myself drank tea and wondered how we had survived the previous two weeks. It seemed as if a lifetime had passed in two weeks. We had assimilated so much and had already formed a new pattern for our existence.

We were very disappointed and sad. Words could never convey what we felt for ourselves, Kelli and Gillian.

The genetic defect existed in both of us so there was no question of it being anyone's fault. We were very sad that night. I cried for the first time. The numbness I had felt since 16th June melted into dreadful sorrow. We allowed ourselves the luxury of showing our feelings for a few days and going over the whole thing constantly.

We were both quite sensible and well balanced people and we quickly made a decision. Brendan said to me one evening as we walked on Bray beach, "Look Ron, it's happened, there is nothing we can do to change that fact. We can fall apart and cry for the rest of our lives, and make a bigger mess of things if we wish. It's up to us, it's our life and our problem and no-one else will really care or understand. On the other hand, we can face the problem head on and fight it to survive. We have to accept that Gillian will die at an early age but no-one knows when. It's when people don't accept things they crack up."

That summer's evening in July 1982 we made a conscious decision. Cystic fibrosis was not going to control our lives, at least not at this early stage. We had two lovely children, a good marriage, nice home and a lot more than many people. Gillian had a serious medical problem but she was being treated for it. Both of us would do our utmost to fight this disease every step of the way. It seemed at that stage it could be many years before it would be a serious worry, little did we know.

Brendan commented, "We have the extra burden of knowing a little too much. There are many people we know to-night who think they have healthy children. Unfortunately, some of those children could die before Gillian but they just don't have the insight into the future we have."

We decided to turn that insight to our own advantage to enrich our lives. Time was now of the utmost importance to us. As a family we wanted to enjoy our children to capacity and make the most of every single day we were all together. If we could have seen the complete picture of the next eight years, that night, would we have been as philosophical?

We talked ourselves into a situation, whereby we felt we could make everything work out by taking it step by step, day by day. We knew that our own relationship would help us through, there was total commitment on both sides, lots of love, and we could communicate well. It would be a team effort and this is where our strength lay. If we did our very best in each situation we would encounter, we felt that was all that was required of anyone in this life. We endeavoured to keep a sense of humour. This discussion was really only a verbalising of what we already thought and were already doing in our daily lives before the tragic revelation of 16th June.

It was in this very positive frame of mind we embarked on the summer. We were really so relieved to have Gillian home and apparently well for the present. Enjoyment of each day was on top of the agenda for us. Gillian and Kelli played out on the street with all the other children and things seemed well. The family went off on picnics to our favourite haunts on Sundays and Mondays. The Powerscourt Waterfall, Brittas Bay and Lough Dan were among our favourite places. We regained a certain amount of our former normality, the only difference being the hour and a half of physiotherapy and extra pills for Gillian every day. Life was fine.

However, two weeks later we received a letter. It was from the consultant and read:

*Dear Mr & Mrs Staunton,*

*Gillian's sputum grew Pseudomonas. This bacteria cannot be treated with an oral antibiotic. I would like you to meet me in the lobby of Harcourt Street at 10 o'clock on Wednesday. I will admit her for another course of IV antibiotics and try and clear it up.*

We didn't know the significance of Gillian already having Pseudomonas! and no-one in the medical world was about to tell us.
I believe, in days gone by, Pseudomonas was an instant death sentence. However, as the stronger IV drugs became available the outlook improved and it could be treated for a time. The prognosis depended on how well the drugs worked and how quickly the bacteria raged through the lung tissue causing permanent damage. Apparently the Pseudomonas causes on-going progressive damage all the time, but it depends on the particular person how quickly it does its deadly deed. It is said that all cystics develop this bacteria eventually, but for many it is not until they are much older.
Anyway, once it colonises in a cystic lung it is almost impossible to eradicate and it can only be controlled at best.
It is my opinion Gillian never had a chance because she developed this awful Pseudomonas so early. We just thought it meant more inconvenience because it had to be treated in hospital, while other cystics were treated with oral drugs at home. If we had been thinking, we would have known that if it needed strong IV drugs to control it, obviously it was serious. Nothing was explained to us.
We now knew there would be more hospitalisation, earlier than other children with cystic fibrosis because of PSEUDOMONAS.
The second hospitalisation wasn't as traumatic as the first time. We were familiar with the treatment and the whole routine of the place. We had recovered a little from the shock of the diagnosis, although still fighting within ourselves to accept it.
The car went back and forth to the hospital twice a day and we brought Gillian in this, that and the other every time we visited. Drinks, food, sweets, yogurt, fruit, little toys or books. We discovered how fast we were spending money and going over our budget. At the time of the first hospitalisation, we hadn't noticed,

as we were in shock. It began to dawn on us that having a child in hospital was an expensive business and threw off the whole family budget. Sometimes Kelli would come in with us and wait in the lobby and she would look for extra drinks and sweets.

During the first hospitalisation we had met a nice priest, who informed us, "You are going to find having a sick child an extra burden financially as well as everything else over the coming months and years. There is financial help available and you are going to need it for the child and it's not means tested."

He told us how to apply to the Eastern Health Board for the Domiciliary or Constant Care Allowance. We barely listened to him and didn't really understand what he meant. We couldn't even think about money those first few weeks after Gillian was diagnosed.

However, during the second hospitalisation in as many weeks, we began to realise it was going to cost a lot of money to look after a constantly sick child. We were grateful to the priest for giving us the information.

I applied to the Eastern Health Board for this monthly allowance of £55. This was available to children over the age of two years, who by virtue of their on-going long-term illness required significantly more care and attention than was usually required for a child of similar age. I also applied for a "green book" for Gillian which was available for certain prescribed, usually terminal, long-term illnesses requiring extensive drugs and medications on an on-going basis. Cystic fibrosis was one of the listed diseases.

I remember reading, at a later date, Margaret McStay's book *Colin* where she described how she couldn't get the green book for her son Colin, who had a liver disease, because his illness was so rare it was not listed! In fact, she seems to have had a very difficult time even getting a medical card for little Colin. I remember thinking at least we were spared the hassle and worry over the payment of

Gillian's drugs. I didn't know the McStays or anything about the Eastern Health Board at that time, but reading Margaret's book I had found it difficult to believe that a Health Board could have been so difficult and lacking in understanding to any family with a very sick child. Today I believe and understand every word Margaret McStay said in her book.

The green book for the drugs arrived very quickly and there was no problem with that. However, the Domiciliary Allowance was not as easy. Many weeks and many phone calls later we received it. Soon after we had applied for it, a lady knocked on our side door one bright sunny day.

She said to Brendan, "I'm from the Eastern Health Board. I've come to see the sick child who you have applied for the Domiciliary Allowance for."

"She's out for a walk with her mother," replied Brendan.

The lady responded, " I thought she was very sick."

Brendan was surprised by her attitude and tone. "Well, she has cystic fibrosis if you know what that is. However, the problem is in her lungs not her legs. No-one said she couldn't go out for a walk on a sunny day."

She told Brendan to tell me to take the baby to the clinic in the Health Centre at 3 o'clock that day for them to see her.

That was our first dealing with the Eastern Health Board.

Gillian came home from hospital for the second time and remained well for the rest of the summer. I phoned my cousin whose little boy of Kelli's age had cystic fibrosis. She was surprised when I told her about Gillian. I had not seen Bernie since my wedding nine years previously. I knew about Barrett having cystic fibrosis, because when I was pregnant with Kelli he was born and was very sick as a baby. My mother had written to me in New York and told me Bernie Moriarty had a lovely little baby boy, but he had this terrible disease and wouldn't live long. She said it was something in herself and her husband that had caused the problem, and the poor baby had to have the back banged off him for hours every day. I remember thinking briefly, that's terrible and then carrying on with what I was doing. Although I was pregnant myself I never dreamed of anything being wrong with this baby or any other we might have in the future. It really is always someone else's problem and until it hits home none of us even really register the horror of other people's problems. I had never phoned Bernie to ask about her child and wouldn't have phoned that day if Gillian had been alright.

Bernie and myself chatted and compared notes about the children. She said Barrett was five and had not been in hospital since he was a baby. She did the physiotherapy three times every day and had to watch fats, because he seemed to be worse in the digestive system. He had nearly died as a baby but made a great recovery and was quite well. This gave me hope for Gillian, after all she had never been close to death. However, when I mentioned Gillian having Pseudomonas, Bernie's voice changed. "No, Barrett doesn't have Pseudomonas," she replied, not elaborating. I asked her lots of questions and we agreed to stay in touch..

Having heard about the *Cystic Fibrosis Association* I also phoned them for a little support and information. I spoke to a Mrs Maguire and I told her about Gillian been diagnosed as having cystic fibrosis. She said maybe she could meet me and have a chat. I said, "That would be great." She took my name and address and said she would be in touch. I never heard any more about meeting me, but a few pamphlets giving information about cystic fibrosis arrived in the post a week later.

We were glad we were living in Ireland rather than America because we knew Gillian would have a better chance to survive. In America there was no free drug scheme for children with cystic fibrosis. Although we were very comfortable in America, we would

never have been able to afford to pay for the very expensive antibiotics and medicine Gillian received here. We had already discovered what our reason for returning to live in Ireland was.
In spite of everything we really enjoyed our summer and Gillian and Kelli grew more lovely by the day. We decided it's not what happens to you in this life that's significant but what you do with what happens!

*Gillian (3 years) with Kelli (6 years).*

# 3. Portugal

It had all started for us on a beautiful sunny summer's evening, 26th May 1980. Brendan and myself headed out of Bray in great form. Our destination, Holles Street Maternity Hospital in Dublin. We expected to be returning home a few days later with a beautiful healthy addition to our family. This was to be our Irish baby. We considered ourselves very lucky to be having this baby at all. Kelli-Ann had been born in New York three years previously, after three miscarriages and a stormy pregnancy. This pregnancy had also been stormy in the beginning. I had already spent a week in Holles Street, in the third month of the pregnancy, as I had suffered from a condition called hyperemesis and had lost two stone in weight from constant vomiting. A deep desire to have a companion for Kelli was the main reason I had gone through another difficult pregnancy.

It was almost over now, and within weeks we would be getting ready to go off to live in Portugal for a few years. The previous summer we had spent ten weeks in Florida. We had lived in a small apartment on Hollywood Beach, almost forty minutes from Miami. It had been a beautiful summer, which we had spent together with Kelli, swimming, reading, talking, eating steak and pizza, and generally enjoying the sunshine and just being together.

We knew that summer Kelli-Ann, who was two years and three months, desperately needed a companion. Gillian was to be that companion!

Although we had lived in New York for many years, we had never become citizens. We had returned to Ireland to live when Kelli was five months old. We felt it was a finer place, with a better quality of life to raise a family. But of course, things are never as straight forward as they seem and we encountered many problems, adjusting to our native country. We ended up emotionally torn between the two countries, in a vacuum not knowing how we would ever settle down. If we could have had the benefits of both countries together, in one place, we would have been satisfied.

As neither Brendan or myself had ever become American citizens, we had returned once a year to keep our Green Cards open, until we settled or went back. This Florida summer was one of such trips, the last in fact, as I returned from my summer in Florida pregnant with Gillian.

During the latter weeks of the pregnancy, we had made arrangements to go off to live in Portugal for a few years as we were still unsettled, but felt returning to America was not our destiny. Each time we returned to America the same problems we had left originally were still there in abundance. The very fast, dangerous pace of life and constant fear of walking around. So we felt two years in Europe, in a nice climate wouldn't be amiss, before Kelli started school. Perhaps it would be the breaker between U.S.A. and Ireland, and it was.

So we were in high spirits that evening in May as we approached Holles Street Maternity Hospital. We had even stopped for a meal in the Montrose Hotel. However, Brendan's after dinner pint was spoilt by me clutching my tummy every two minutes as the pains got closer.

Gillian came quietly into the world a few hours later, 12.10 a.m. on 27th May 1980. She was pronounced healthy but, of course, she wasn't. Three days later Kelli, with her big blue eyes and blond curly hair, got her first glimpse of her new sister, who in contrast to herself had very straight dark hair and dark eyes.

I think Kelli thought she was going to have an instant playmate, and seemed quite disappointed Gillian seemed to be sleeping most of the time. The day after Gillian came home from hospital

Kelli brought about ten children into our front room "to see her new sister".

We had found it difficult before the birth to decide on a girl's name. My hairdresser at the time had a baby girl called Gillian. I asked her if she would mind us calling our baby Gillian, if we had a girl. She said, "Not at all", Susan asked me to phone and let her know when I had the baby. So, a week or so after I came home I phoned to tell her we also had a Gillian. Her sister answered the phone and when I delivered my message for Susan she said, "Did you not hear our bad news?" I said, "What do you mean?" "Susan's baby Gillian died, it was a cot death."

She asked me what date our Gillian was born and when I said, "27th May", she said, "That's the date we lost our Gillian."

I was absolutely shocked and a shiver went up my spine. I'm not superstitious, but I must admit feeling strange about this incident. After I told Brendan, I said, "Will we change the name?" But we decided we were being silly. We felt very sorry for Susan, especially as it was her first baby. I felt it was an omen of impending disaster.

When Gillian was three weeks old she started to cough, it was a funny little cough accompanied by a clear runny nose. It was strange because the weather was good and it was a funny time for colds. We sent for the doctor when the cough persisted for a day or two. So at three weeks Gillian went on her first antibiotic. The little cough stopped and we didn't dwell on it. She was feeding well, in fact too well, she always seemed to be hungry. After feeding her myself for six weeks I stopped because she was drinking a bottle of milk straight after feeding from me, such was her appetite. I decided I couldn't possibly compete. At six weeks she again needed antibiotics as the cough was back. It seemed we had a chesty baby.

We continued with our plans to go away, renting the house etc. Two days before we were due to leave for Portugal, Gillian's cough was back. The doctor came again and said she would give her another antibiotic, as we were embarking on such a long journey.

The night before we left, Gillian's godparents, John and Bernie Galvin came out to help Brendan pack the play-pen, cot and pram on the roof-rack of the car.

I remember clearly, John, who is very conservative, looking at the 1973 yellow Cortina laden down with gear, then looking at us. He tilted his head and said, "Well Ron and Brendan you really are going off, fair play to you, good luck now."

I said, "John you think we're cracked, don't you?" He did, but he was much too polite to say so.

We set off in high spirits the next morning. This was to be our last adventure. Little did we know within a year we would be back in Bray and would do very little travelling for a very long time!

Ten days later we arrived in Lisbon, Portugal to begin what was going to be an interesting year in many ways. We found a lovely apartment about a seven minute walk from the seaside resort of Cascais, half an hour from the city of Lisbon.

It was very different from our three bedroom semi-detached house in Bray. Our apartment was one flight up a white marble stairs and the building had about ten apartments in it. The complex of about fifteen apartment buildings had a coffee shop and several other shops. It was quite self-contained with even a playground with swings for children.

Three year old Kelli delighted in going downstairs, locking herself out of the building and then ringing the bell to get back in. We found out more about Kelli through this new experience of travelling. She wasn't as adaptable as we had always thought young children were. From the day we left Bray to travel to Portugal she kept insisting she wanted to go home to Bray. For the first three days of the journey Kelli-Ann would not eat. Finally on the fourth day Brendan and herself had an awful row in the middle of Spain.

"Why won't you eat Kelli?" asked Brendan.

"I won't eat until I get home to Woodbrook Lawn and my friend Grainne," she replied.

"Well love, you'll have a long wait, two years is no long weekend."

He got quite cross with her and finally she relented and ate a little, but she was much lighter when we arrived in Portugal than the day we left home.

September in Lisbon was a beautiful sunny month. Cascais is in an idyllic setting, sea, sand, sun and lots of very inexpensive good restaurants. We were as happy as any family could be. Kelli was lovely and now our beautiful baby Gillian was our icing on the cake. After three miscarriages we considered ourselves blessed.

I was teaching in St. Dominic's International School, as were three other Irish teachers. It was an exclusive private school run by the Dominican Nuns. The school was about five miles along the coast from our apartment. Kelli and myself drove there each morning as I had enrolled Kelli in the pre-school class in the school.

Brendan walked the ten minute journey down to the Hotel Citadel where he was cutting hair. Marie, a young Portuguese girl of about twenty, looked after Gillian in the apartment. I remember the first day Marie came to work for us. I phoned at lunch time to see if all was well at home. Marie answered the phone and said "Senior Brendan out, Madam Veronica is at school." I said, "Hello Marie, this is Veronica." To which she again replied, "Madam Veronica is at school." No matter what I said she kept repeating this like a parrot. In the end I gave up and said, "I am Madam Veronica. Goodbye."

Marie would look after Gillian, clean the apartment and even offered to cook. After experiencing one of her greasy Spanish omelettes, I declined her offer to cook. I told her it was quite alright if she just tidied up and took care of the baby.

Every evening after work we would set off walking down to Cascais, pushing Gillian in her buggy over the cobbled pavement. The palm trees lined the road. It was a quaint little place, a mixture of old and new. We were even able to spend some time on the beach during September. The children really enjoyed these hours, Kelli making sand castles and paddling in the clear blue water and Gillian, who was beginning to crawl, experiencing the taste of sand and the joy of the soft silvery sand slipping through her toes and fingers. She would gurgle with delight as she pushed herself along in the sand. Kelli quickly acquired a suntan, which highlighted her blue eyes and curly hair. Gillian was thriving, really thriving – suntanned, chubby, big brown eyes and a bit of straight dark hair on the top of her head. She could have been a boy but the face was much too pretty.

There are things, times and places in everyone's life which are always in our memory for whatever emotions they evoke.

That particular September of 1980 is one we will remember forever. It was Brendan's first experience of a European country, as he had left Galway at eighteen to live in America, having lost his mother at the age of twelve. He was savouring every minute of his new life. We would sit out on the balcony of our apartment in the evening when the children were asleep and talk for hours. We ate lots of chicken, which had a delicious flavour of its own. Brendan said the Portuguese chicken reminded him of Irish untampered chicken of the fifties. In fact, Portugal in 1980 was very like Ireland of the fifties and the people reminded us of the Irish people. They were a sentimental people, who loved children, with a very easy-going personality. Compulsory car insurance had only recently been introduced!

The Portuguese around the world are compared to the Spanish people because they are neighbours, as the Irish and English are linked together in other parts of the world. The same animosity existed to this linkage between both Portuguese and Spanish as with the Irish and English people. We found this very amusing. Brendan would often say to a Portuguese person, "Spain and Portugal similar, yes?" Instantly they would reply, "No, no, not so. Spain no good." He would laugh.

Groups of men would gather together and play pitch and toss for hours and hours and afterwards retire to the coffee shop to drink black coffee, beer or brandy. Brendan got a kick out of observing all of this and said it reminded him so much of Ireland in the '50s. My own family had been victims of sickness and unemployment in the Ireland of the 1950s. I had left Ireland in 1954 at the age of eight. I remember vividly heading off from Dun Laoghaire on the boat to Holyhead en-route to a new life in London, with a big doll in my arms, a school bag on my back and a beret from St. David's School in Greystones on my head. This is how I arrived in London, where no-one could understand what I was saying for a while, due to my strong Irish accent. To me it was all a big adventure and I became very adaptable. Not so my parents, who always hankered after Ireland and in fact returned twelve years later, when I was away at Teacher Training College in London. I had not really remembered much about the Ireland of the '50s. When my parents returned to live in Ireland in 1965 I began to spend more time here, it was a very different country to the pre-television days of the early '50s.

On the other hand, Brendan had spent all of his first eighteen years in Annaghdown in Co. Galway. He came from a farming background, being the youngest of eight. He inherited his father, Pat's, musical talent and was an accomplished traditional accordionist by the age of seven. Hence his great interest in comparing Portugal of 1980 with Ireland of the 1950s. He took a great interest in the Portuguese traditional or Fado music. In New York he had worked as a full time musician for many years. Within a month of living in Lisbon, he had advertised his musical ability in the local paper for English speaking people. He quickly started getting gigs, private parties and functions to play and his music was very much appreciated in Lisbon. Soon he was playing their own Fado music, mixed in with the Irish traditional, Scottish and anything else in demand. Sometimes I would go along and enjoy the musical evening, and other times I would stay home with the children. Hairdressing, playing music and teaching kept us all very busy. We were very happy although Kelli still spoke of Bray constantly and kept asking, "When are we going home?" Because there were four of us on the staff from Ireland it was easier to keep up with the news from home.

Suddenly, one evening in October Gillian began to cough and she coughed and coughed and coughed and went purple in the face. She coughed continuously all through the night. We sat up with her and were unable to do anything to ease her stress. We tried to get an English speaking doctor but without success. We attempted to contact the English Hospital in Lisbon but could not get any reply. The isolation we felt that night, and frustration by lack of knowledge of the language was immense.

I thought that night Gillian would die and we were so helpless. The poor little thing looked so tiny and fragile. At 8 o'clock in the morning, a doctor who spoke English arrived. He said Gillian had bronchitis and would grow out of it when she was around two. He gave us an antibiotic and told us to give her a five day course of it whenever the cough came back. He also told us to keep her warm. We were already keeping heat on all night for her, because I had noticed every time the temperature in the room dropped she would cough and the nose would run. The experience was frightening and we weren't really convinced the doctor was right, but the antibiotic worked almost immediately so we were happy and relaxed a little. So Gillian was a chesty baby, not an uncommon condition and she now had a little bronchitis.

Christmas came and went and it just didn't have the Christmas atmosphere, and it didn't seem right to be sitting out on a veranda in sunshine on Christmas Day. In fact, construction workers worked away on a building down the road. We missed Ireland a little but made the best of things. One of the Irish teachers from Donegal had her mother out for a few months, so we invited them to join us for dinner and I cooked a turkey. Eithna and Mrs McFadden enjoyed the day but we all agreed it just wasn't the same in the sun. Ireland is very special at Christmas and we were sorry to be away.

By February we were once again able to walk on the beaches and sit outside coffee shops in the evenings. In fact, we spent a Sunday afternoon on the very sandy Guincho beach about five miles further along the coast from Cascais. It was unthinkable in Ireland in February to spend an afternoon on the beach. It was during this particular Sunday afternoon, an incident happened which was significant but we didn't know it at the time. Gillian was eating an ice-cream, a little piece of ice-cream fell on her arm. I licked her arm to remove the ice-cream and instead of a sweet taste I was left with a terrible salty taste in my mouth. This is a symptom of cystic fibrosis, but I didn't know it!

Approaching St. Patrick's Day, Brendan was very much in demand with his Irish music. He played all over Lisbon at private parties. I was at one party with him and he was highly embarrassed when a hoola hoop competition was announced and I entered and won.

We became friendly with the first secretary to the Irish Embassy, Jim Brennan and his wife Jean, as I was teaching their daughter Fiona. I would often have lunch with Jean and we were invited to several dinners at their home with Mr Kirwan, the Irish Ambassador in Lisbon.

There were only seventy Irish people in Lisbon so it was always the same people one would meet at social gatherings. It was all very enjoyable for a while. Everyone talked a lot about Ireland.

Our life in Portugal was very different from our life in either New York or Ireland. It was a nice interlude between the two. We felt lucky to have had the opportunity to live in Europe for a while and would like to have stayed for the two years. However, our increasing doubts about Gillian's health prompted us to make the decision to return to Ireland after one year. We felt if her health was to deteriorate we should be home, where there was some chance that the root of the problem could be found. If the wind blew or the temperature dropped, Gillian coughed! I felt if I could wrap her up and keep her very warm for ever and protect her from the elements she would be fine. Having been a chesty baby myself and having grown out of it, we didn't really worry very seriously at that stage. It never crossed our mind it was anything fatal. We thought if we returned home it could be diagnosed.

So, we would leave Portugal, and return in mid-August when our house would be free to move back into, having rented it for a year. We set out to enjoy the summer and expose Gillian to as much sunshine as possible for her chest.

Brendan was playing music five nights a week that summer, so the hairdressing was put on hold until we returned home. I was off on holidays from school and our days were spent together at the beach. It was a fabulous summer, really lovely. It was like an extended holiday in the sun, a little like the summer in Florida except now we had Gillian. She had just passed her first birthday and Kelli was finding her more interesting. They played in the sand and developed lovely suntans. Gillian was very quiet and let Kelli pull her around and bury her in the sand with just her head sticking out. Gillian started to walk at nine months, so by that summer she was very steady on her feet and ran all over the beach, tipping her toes in the cold clear water and running away.

We would come home from the beach in the evening and shower, have a nice family meal and Brendan would go off to work in the

English club he had been working in since April. I would play with the children and read them stories when they were ready for bed. The two were just gorgeous, Kelli at four with a big head of blonde curls, big blue eyes and tanned skin, and Gillian at just one year, straight dark hair, very dark tan and huge brown eyes, set in a small chubby face. She always had a calm gentleness about her. I would read when the children went to bed and wait for Brendan to come home. We would drink tea and chat about his night in "Deus Pedros". The customers were mainly English people on holiday in Mont Estoril. It was truly a very nice time in our lives. As soon as Brendan came home every night he would give me a peck on the cheek and immediately open the bedroom doors just to look at the two children sleeping peacefully. He would say, "Aren't they lovely?" His two children were a great source of joy to his life.

As the summer went by we began to get a little apprehensive about the long journey back over the mountains of Portugal and up through France. Would our old Cortina make it? Also, we had been in Lisbon nearly a year and we had never made a trip to Fatima, which was about one hundred miles away.

"We really should see Fatima before we go home," I said to Brendan, "We might never be out this way again and it's so close, it might be nice to take Gillian."

The next day we set off and stayed overnight in Fatima. A beautiful uncommercial spot set high in the mountains. I was glad we went and I prayed that Gillian would be alright.

All too soon it was time to put the roof rack on the Cortina for the seven or eight days' drive to Ireland. We were dreading the journey, but decided it would be best to try and make a little holiday of it. We had picnics on the side of the road in France once we were through Portugal and Spain. The yellow Cortina held up well.

Amazingly, the summer in the sun had helped Gillian and for some reason she seemed quite well. The coughing had stopped. We had enjoyed the year and after that we rarely spoke much about America. In some ways the pace of life in Portugal had been slower than Ireland and certainly at a standstill compared to New York. It had been the breaker we had hoped for. We settled quite easily in Ireland after Portugal. It was now four years since we had left New York.

Brendan set up a room in the house to work from, while he looked for a suitable shop to open his "Hair Studio". I went substitute teaching and within eight weeks or so, had a permanent teaching post in an inner city school. My parents were happy we were back, as I think they had missed the children, and Brendan's Dad in Galway was glad we had returned. In fact, they all thought there was something wrong with us going off in the first place. We didn't fit into the normal mould!

Gillian remained well as long as the temperature didn't drop down too low. The house was well heated day and night and she was well wrapped whenever she went out. A week before Christmas she got a bad throat infection and the doctor came. I said to the doctor, "She wouldn't have cystic fibrosis would she doctor?"

I don't know why I said that or really why it crossed my mind.

She said I was fussing and responded, "Look, she's a fine thriving baby. Cystic fibrosis children don't thrive like that."

I was reassured, but still asked for a letter for a consultant. The letter for the consultant remained in my bag for some time.

In early January of 1982 we were snowed in for several days, and people had to be air lifted out of many places. Gillian's throat infection cleared and we didn't think about the consultant for a while.

The weather was bad that winter and we were all busy surviving the elements. She hardly went outside the door those few months after Christmas. However, by early March she had to go on another antibiotic for her cough. I made an appointment for the consultant and saw him in Sir Patrick Dunne's Hospital in April.
The antibiotic had cleared her up again and he could find little wrong with her. He kept asking about Kelli and I said Kelli had been very healthy. He was very interested in Gillian's bowel movements, which were normal. Obviously he suspected cystic fibrosis to some extent. He said he didn't think it was anything serious but he would like to run a few tests on her over in Harcourt Street Hospital and would let us have an appointment shortly. Weeks went by and we heard nothing from the doctor, which re-assured us. He wasn't very worried.
In late May around her second birthday the cough was back and I said,"She's not going on any more antibiotics until he sees her."
I phoned and asked for the appointment which I got for June 10th. The rest is history.

*Kelli and Gillian making daisy-chains (1983)*

# *4. Living with Cystic Fibrosis 1982-86*

After much soul-searching that summer we had decided I would continue teaching. Many factors contributed to that decision, one being I enjoyed teaching, and to get up in the morning and go off to a job would, we felt, help me to cope with Gillian's illness. I knew that I was capable of switching off from my personal problems and for five hours every day I could forget cystic fibrosis and keep it a separate part of my life, and this I felt would help us keep things as normal as possible.

Gillian still looked very well and we had no reason to suppose we could not lead a near normal life for many years, and of course we thought they would probably have a cure for cystic fibrosis within a few years. The significance of Pseudomonas did not sink in, maybe subconsciously we didn't want to know. We were doing physiotherapy three times a day as instructed by the hospital. We thought Gillian was only mildly affected by cystic fibrosis or so we convinced ourselves. We had recovered a little from the shock of the diagnosis by September. Many discussions had taken place over the summer and we had come to terms with the fact that we could not expect a completely normal life any more, but would do our utmost to have as close to a normal existence as the disease would allow.

I knew that for me to continue working and travelling into Dublin every day I would need an awful lot of support from Brendan. When we returned from Portugal he had set up a small men's hair studio in the house while he looked for a suitable shop in the town. We decided he would continue working from the house for a while until Gillian was a little older and went to school. This took the pressure off me. I went off to my teaching job in Dublin every day leaving Brendan to do Gillian's physiotherapy, look after her and work from his hair studio. If he wasn't busy he would also cook dinner and have it ready when I arrived home at 3.30 p.m.

Often Brendan would be cutting hair until 10 o'clock at night. Men would come around after dinner to have their hair cut and seemed to enjoy the service. Sometimes he would do a few cuts during the day and after dinner we would take the children for a walk on Bray beach, leaving a note on the door that he would be back in half an hour. We all really enjoyed these outings and to look at Gillian no one would have known there was anything wrong. We lived very much in the present. Because Brendan was working from the house, he liked to go out on Sundays, so, usually we would go off for a drive in the country and end up having tea out somewhere. Everything we did was very family orientated. There was a tight schedule and we were very organised. At night we went to bed as early as possible because Gillian always woke up during the night. She had never slept through a night since she was born.

Brendan would say, "If we get four or five hours sleep before she wakes, we'll be okay". Sometimes she would wake coughing, other times just crying.

It is amazing how one can adjust to anything. The physiotherapy had become a part of our daily life and we did it automatically. Brendan did the morning and mid-day shift and I did the night shift. Kelli wondered why this pounding of Gillian's back and sides had to go on three times a day. She thought at first we were hitting the child. However, the benefits of the treatment were obvious and Gillian herself knew she felt better after it, so she never complained.

As time went by and Gillian was able to speak she asked why we had to do this thing every day. I just said, "Gillian, you have a lung disease called cystic fibrosis and this treatment will help you breathe easier and make you feel better." She knew this was true so she accepted everything. She took the pills to help her digest her food because we told her these would also help her. In these early years Gillian was very quiet, pleasant and placid. She just needed plenty of love. If you sat her on your knee and cuddled her she would have been happy to sit there all day.

In January 1983, six months after Gillian was diagnosed, I changed jobs. I was extremely lucky to secure a teaching post in St. Patrick's Loreto Primary School in Bray, a five minute drive from our house. It looked as if things were going our way. On my first day in St. Patrick's, I met Una McCabe, who was to become a close friend in the difficult years ahead. The school was very big, with almost a thousand children and thirty staff. Una's classroom was just down the corridor from mine. On my first day she said, "If you want to know anything just ask me". I hope she is not sorry she gave me such an invitation. I took her at her word and kept popping in and out of her classroom when I needed to know anything.

I didn't tell anyone about Gillian at the beginning. Una says I was very jolly, friendly and out-going and no one would have known there was a thing wrong in my life. In fact, she said she was very surprised when she heard I had a child with cystic fibrosis.

Our life seemed to be under control and jogging along on an even keel. We were cautiously optimistic that Gillian could grow up. Brendan preferred not to talk about cystic fibrosis too much. We carried out the necessary daily treatment and other than that, he wanted to forget it had entered our lives.

His father and brother lived in Galway and my parents and brother lived in Bray. Other than that, we had few friends as we had been away so long. I had some good friends in England and we both had friends in America. Brendan didn't want to bother his aging father too much with our problem and always kept up a good front when he saw his Dad. My parents were supportive and were always willing to baby-sit and do whatever they could for us. However, I never wanted them to see how really devastated we were inside over Gillian. I feel older people should not have to be burdened too much with their children's problems. You leave the nest as an adult and should be mature enough to cope with your own life and what it brings, good or bad. Older people who have raised their family should be left in peace to do their own thing and enjoy their latter years.

So, together with our two young children we adjusted to cystic fibrosis and hoped things would be alright. We are both independent, self-sufficient, private people who don't need many people outside ourselves to be happy. We don't really enjoy large social gatherings. In the first year of living with cystic fibrosis the only outings we had were as a family. The children went everywhere with us. Any social contact I had was mainly the staff at school who were all new to me. I am an extrovert by nature and chatted to many people about a lot of topics but as time went by I became more friendly with Una.

When I took Gillian for a check-up to Harcourt Street, I would always try to quiz the doctor about her condition. I would say things like, "How do you think she is going doctor, doesn't she look well?"

One day he looked at me and said. "Yes, she is well today." In other words, don't ask beyond today.

No one would or could tell me she would live a long happy life, simply because she had cystic fibrosis!

Sometimes the phlegm she would cough up from the physiotherapy would be green and an antibiotic would be prescribed, and within a week or two the mucus coughed up would be white and clear again. Whenever a sputum was cultured it always grew Pseudomonas because once this bacteria colonises in a cystic lung it cannot be eradicated, but only controlled. When the growth grew heavy, IV antibiotics were necessary. We only began to understand the significance of Gillian having Pseudomonas as time went by. No one told us how serious it was to have Pseudomonas already at two years of age. I read the pamphlets sent by the Cystic Fibrosis Association and saw how closely the sputum was being monitored. I also thought back to the reactions of my cousin who has a cystic fibrosis child, when I mentioned Pseudomonas and of a neighbour with two cystic fibrosis children. My cousin said Barrett, her little boy, didn't have Pseudomonas, and the neighbour said her child didn't get it until she was eight. Within the first year, Gillian was hospitalised twice apart from the initial hospitalisation. She was given two weeks of IV gentamycin each time for the Pseudomonas. She still looked well, ate well and seemed to be making good progress and had plenty of energy.

By her third birthday Gillian was playing out on the street with Kelli and all the other children. I always had her well dressed, with extra jumpers to keep her warm, otherwise she looked the same as everyone else. Dr. Doyle came to the house once to see Brendan and said, "It's good you are letting Gillian out with the kids, she seems to be enjoying herself. I'm glad you are not being over protective towards her."

In June 1983, just after her third birthday, Gillian and myself spent four days in Lourdes with the Cystic Fibrosis Association. I met a girl with whom I subsequently became friends. Irene Walsh from the north side of Dublin had a lovely little boy, Sean, who was just a little younger than Gillian. I would say on that trip Sean and Gillian looked chubby, well and healthy. Thankfully Sean has remained well and has had very little IV drugs until this past year.

We pushed the two children all over Lourdes in their buggies and talked a lot about our short experience of cystic fibrosis. Some of the other children on the trip were skinny and sick looking and some were sporting a cannula, which is a yellow bung on the end of a needle to keep the vein open in their arms for the IV drugs. Irene and myself felt lucky our children looked so well.

However, that trip to Lourdes taught me a lot I didn't want to know. I came down to breakfast in the hotel one morning and overheard a conversation between three women who were getting acquainted. They were very casually discussing their experience of cystic fibrosis. One said to the other, "Yes, this is my third with it, I lost the other two a few years ago, went very quick in the end both of them."

"Well, I've two alive and well so far. I just lost a baby seven years ago, awful bloody disease." At that point I'd heard enough and didn't feel hungry any more. I made a quick exit from the dining-room.

By and large, I saw and heard too much during those few days and was glad to get home. Gillian came home with a dreadful chest infection and was admitted to Harcourt Street the following weekend. Brendan said, "Well Ron, Lourdes didn't do you much good and that child went away well and came back sick."

July 1983 was the turning point for Gillian, one year after the diagnosis. She came home from hospital and from that day on her phlegm was a horrible green colour and it never became clear again until June 1990. The IV treatment did little for her. She became very productive and brought up an awful lot of green phlegm every time she had physiotherapy. The little girl never seemed to have a lot of energy after that fateful summer.

That summer Gillian played on the street with all the children, but now she coughed more and tired easily. She came in more often to rest for a while and then would trot off again to join in the fun. She loved to run and was a fast runner, but running always made her cough. There were the usual family picnics at Brittas Bay and the Powerscourt Waterfall. Monday was our favourite day. Brendan worked all day Saturday and took Sunday and Monday off. The beaches and Waterfall were nice and quiet on a Monday. As long as the sun was shining we were off. This part of our lives would have been the same even if Gillian had not been ill but the knowledge we now had just heightened our appreciation of each sunny beautiful day we spent enjoying ourselves as a family. Kelli knew Gillian better than anyone in the world because they shared a bedroom and each other's lives. I will let Kelli talk a little about how Gillian was in those early years.

## Kelli's Contribution

*When Gillian and I were small we would always play games in our back garden in Woodbrook Lawn, it was our favourite place to play games because it was big with loads of trees and flowers. We would sit down on a rug and have a picnic. We would put on make-up and my mother's clothes and pretend we were rich princesses having our lunch. Gillian loved flowers and she would sit in the sun making daisy chains for hours. She loved to play hospital and put drips on her dolls and give them physiotherapy.*

*We shared a room in our old house and at night time Gillian would tape herself singing songs and she would put on a show for me. She loved to sing and dance. She would pretend to be a pop star. Gillian really enjoyed life and she loved playing outside with the children. Even if she did not have the energy she would force herself and make herself have the ability to do the things that she enjoyed doing. Gillian was totally different from other children. She found children her own age boring and she could not communicate with them. Not just out in the street but when she went to hospital she always became friends with student doctors and they were amazed how mature for her age she was. A lot more mature because of the experience of her illness. She had been through a lot.*

*Gillian loved the sunshine and she would go berserk if it rained. Whenever it was rainy she would try making a magic spell to make the sun come out. She would use shampoo, washing-up liquid, perfume and other liquids and if by coincidence the sun did come out later on, she would go around shouting, "It worked, it worked". Gillian has always loved drama, excitement and adventure and each night she would say to Mum, "What's happening tomorrow?" She loved going places and going out to dinner to her favourite hotel, The Montrose. She also loved walking on the beach at night, Gillian loves going out at night. She loves when people come to visit us and she would show off her dancing talents to them. I remember the way she talked about the cure for cystic fibrosis. She would explain to me what it was going to be like and what it would do to her. She had an image in her head of it. Every night when we were in bed she would remind me to pray for the cure. She would look at the news some nights waiting for them to announce that they had found it. I think as she got older she knew deep down that there was no cure, but needed something to hold on to. Something to give her hope and to help her hang on. I think it was good the way my parents kept telling her that there was a cure coming, because that made her fight.*

*I remember the way my parents could never get Gill to eat her food. Day after day it was a struggle to get her to eat. She just couldn't put it down her, her appetite was gone. She would just sit there shaking her head saying, "No, I'm not hungry". and Dad would say, "Come on pet, eat your dinner, like a good girl". Then she would start crying and a row would have broken out. Mum would shop around spending a bomb on all different types of food for Gill.*

*Christmas time was always her favourite time of the year. She just loved the atmosphere of Christmas. Not just the fact of receiving gifts, but she enjoyed decorating the Christmas tree and going down the town to look at the lights. Mum and Dad used to take us shopping around Dublin in and out of different shops. Gillian loved singing all the songs the shops played. Gillian went through an awful lot with cystic fibrosis. She used to cough constantly and spent months every year in hospital having terrible needles and tubes down her nose. But never in my life did I hear her complain. She made the best out of each day. I admire Gillian for her courage. She is the best sister anyone could have.*

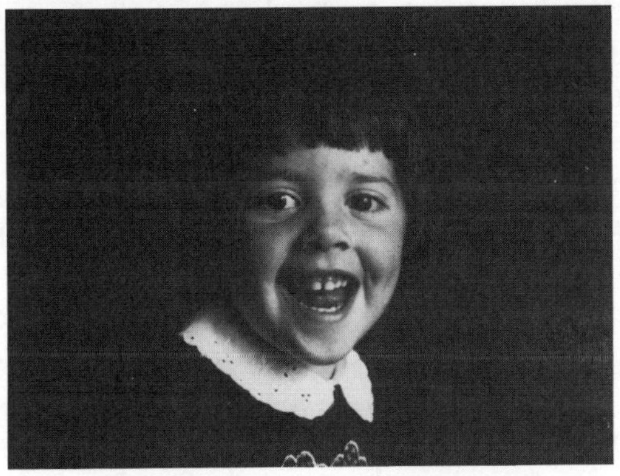

*Gillian (3 years and 5 months)*

We began our second year of living with cystic fibrosis with a deep seated knowledge that Gillian was on a downhill course. No one in the medical profession was saying anything, but instinct and good eyesight told us we were slowly losing the battle, although we didn't want to admit it. In October I asked the consultant how badly she was affected. He just looked at me and I continued, "Mildly affected, moderately or severely?" He replied, "Mild to moderate", and that was supposed to appease me for that day, which it did.

Gillian herself was beginning to ask more questions. One night when I was pounding her back she asked would she have to have this treatment all of her life, I responded, "Until they find the cure for cystic fibrosis." She promptly replied, "Where did they lose it?" I explained as well as one can explain to a child of not yet four years of age what the cure was likely to be. After that she would tell Kelli that one day there would be a cure for her disease. "It might be a little pill I will pop into my mouth, it will go into my tummy and I'll stop coughing and feel better and no more banging everyday, no more hospital and needles. Won't that be great Kelli."

In the meantime the daily drudgery of the treatment continued. She needed longer, more aggressive physiotherapy now to dislodge the thick filthy mucus which impaired her breathing. I firmly believe, had it not been for Brendan's very aggressive physiotherapy that particular year she would have died. He went after the phlegm like a madman because he knew it was building up every few hours and her only hope was to keep it moving. She was hospitalised a good few times during the year for the usual treatment, two weeks IV gentamycin. She still woke up every single night.

During one of these hospitalisations they had terrible trouble getting a vein to house the cannula for the drugs to go through. Her veins were small and they kept collapsing. Sometimes when they would site the needle, it could possibly last for four or five days. Then when it would "tissue", they would maybe find a vein in the other arm and change it over. Other times the vein would only last a day and the prodding of Gillian's arm for another vein would begin again. As soon as we would walk into the ward we would know if the vein had "tissued". Gillian would be lying on the bed holding the sore arm or just quietly crying to herself. On this particular occasion I walked into the treatment room. Five wasted sterile needles lay on the end of the bed to signify five failed attempts to site the needle. The doctor was prodding Gillian's arm with the sixth needle. I couldn't believe this was happening to my four year old child. For the first time I almost despaired. I walked out of the room and met the House Doctor in the corridor.

"This can't continue, I think I will take the child home. She's going through hell."

"But Mrs. Staunton, Gillian needs this treatment to survive". "Yes, to survive for another few months, is it really worth it? She's going through too much for too little."

I was very tired and very disillusioned. At this point Brendan came along. He knew I was very upset.

"Go down and sit in the car for a few minutes Ron. I'll stay with Gillian until they get the needle in her vein." He was always so calm.

This was one of the very few times I showed emotion in the hospital. I sat in the car and the flood gates opened. I just couldn't bear to see her going through so much, it just wasn't fair. While I was sitting in the car a friend of ours from Bray came and joined me. Rosemary had met Brendan on the ward and he told her I was upset. She came and sat beside me in the car and handed me a Novena and said she had just said it for Gillian. Rosemary understood how I felt because her own little boy, Stephen, had leukaemia and they were spending a lot of time in the hospital. We started to talk and joke about the whole thing and I cheered up and we went for coffee. Rosemary and myself were trying to decide which was worse, leukaemia or cystic fibrosis. Six of one and half a dozen of the other was our verdict. Returning to the ward half an hour later Gillian was sitting on Brendan's knee chatting away, her usual cheery self, sporting her yellow cannula in her right fragile arm, "They got a good vein just after you left Mum", she chirped.

In January 1984 my parents took Gillian into the hospital for a check-up. My mother was upset when she came home. She told me the doctor put Gillian's X-ray on the screen and explained it to a group of students. He didn't realise my Mum was watching and he pointed to several parts of the X-ray and shook his head and said Pseudomonas! Her lungs had permanent damage. I couldn't even react to this latest news. When someone you love is constantly sick and constantly having problems, it is impossible to sustain the hurt at a high level for every event. You become used to having problems and hearing bad news over a long period. It's not possible to always react. The result is an on-going numbness that's set at a certain level and some of the bad news and disappointments just bounce off. I just said, "We can only do our best Mum, thanks for taking her in".

As the summer once more approached we began to get very frustrated. Gillian was going downhill, she wasn't eating much, and when she did eat she would often vomit because she would start coughing and it would bring the carefully prepared dinner up over the kitchen floor. It was a vicious circle. When this would happen Brendan and myself would look at each other, one of us would mop up the vomit, the other would prepare something else for the child to eat and we would say "tomorrow is another day, we will start all over and try again."

We both continued working and every spare minute went looking after Gillian. Kelli was getting tired of it all, she was fed up going from pillar to post when we went in and out of the hospital. She was bored waiting in the lobby if she didn't want to stay with my parents or a friend. She saw Gillian taking all the attention in time and energy. One night Gillian woke up coughing and when I had settled her I came back into the room with a drink. Kelli was sitting on Gillian's bed pointing her finger in Gillian's face saying, "You've brought a lot of trouble to this house Gillian Staunton." Gillian just replied, "I'm sorry Kelli." We were beginning to have our strength and endurance tested.

She was such a happy child in spite of everything and this is what made everything so difficult and hard to accept. She gave us so much joy mixed in with all the problems and no matter how sick she was she had the capacity to have the will to enjoy any little outing. Gillian was a good skater at the age of three and we would walk on Bray Beach and the two children would skate like mad along the prom. This exercise would loosen the phlegm and help the physiotherapy. This outing was a special event for Gillian as was any little outing. She had the ability to enjoy life and get something out of every day in spite of her limitations and illness.

In July 1984 as Gillian passed her fourth birthday and we were beginning to get tired and worn out and feel the effects of coping with two years of cystic fibrosis, Gillian once more needed hospitalisation. House doctors changed every six months in the hospital, the 1st January and 1st July. A new chap had just arrived. He innocently handed me Gillian's file and said, "Go on up to the ward and I will meet you up there in fifteen minutes."

"Fine, doctor," I said and headed straight for the coffee shop, to have a look at the file. Brendan said, "Veronica, don't read that file because there is nothing good in it for you to hear and you are better off not knowing." I ignored him and ploughed through it. I didn't have time for much detail but got the gist of things. One letter written after the bad infection following Lourdes read, "Both surprising and very disappointing she did not respond to the treatment." Another part of a letter which made me cross read, "The mother seems to think she is only mildly affected! In spite of being very well looked after and receiving good daily physiotherapy she is not making the progress one would expect." My heart sank because I already knew by looking at Gillian that she was on a downward slide and I resented not being told exactly how my child was. Brendan regarded it as kindness on the doctors' part to withhold information. "In other words," I said, "She will just keep sliding and one day die quietly."

I thought to myself over and over that summer, surely something can be done to stave off this rapid deterioration, other cystic children were living until they were well into their teens, why does our one have to be allowed to keep sliding? I honestly felt the treatment she was receiving was not aggressive enough. Two weeks of gestamycin wasn't good enough.

Reading everything I could get my hands on I noted that some doctors were using nebulizers to inhale antibiotics. I had been observing another younger doctor doing his rounds for quite some time, Dr Brian Denham and often thought he seemed to be a fighter and had a much more aggressive approach to the treatment. He was vibrant, enthusiastic and young. I liked his style. But what could I do? We could hardly change from one doctor to another in the same hospital. Brendan said he had also noticed Dr Brian Denham but it was a tricky one and we shelved it.

Gillian started school in September. A child's first day at school is, I think, always an emotional experience for any mother. Teaching for a long time I've seen many mothers part from their young children for the first time. The Mums are often upset but the children are always very happy once the mother has left the room. If it's the first child or the last the parting is always harder. In any event it's a special day in the child's and the mother's life.

The day Gillian went to school for the first time was very special. It was 2nd September 1984. In spite of her failing health we thought it better to try and get her to school, this was part of keeping things as normal as possible. It was different for me because unlike other mothers I wasn't leaving her, she was now with me in school and I could see her at break time. I was teaching upstairs and at 10.45 a.m. I rushed down just to see her. She was four years and three months, one of the youngest in the class. Walking into the room and looking around at all the lovely little faces it was easy to pick out Gillian. She was smiling like the rest of the children but she looked smaller, paler, thinner and already very tired. I wondered how long she would wear the little wine tunic, tie and V-neck jumper and cream blouse. She wore it three full days and then went into hospital with pneumonia. She had the usual two weeks intravenous antibiotics and came home, to our mind no better than when she went in. She did not return to school again until the following September.

Then something happened in late September to force our hand. I paid a visit to my G.P., Dr Rita Doyle, after Gillian came out of hospital. She handed me a letter from the consultant about Gillian and she said, "Veronica, I know you don't want any shocks."

I read the letter and I felt sick, it was full of medical language describing the lung damage but the one sentence which I will remember forever was: "The prognosis for this child is very poor." He had given up on her. For weeks afterwards I kept waking with this sentence flashing before me. My whole reaction was panic. I immediately changed G.P. to another doctor who was supposed to be very involved in cystic fibrosis. He said the longest she could live was five years no matter what we did, and the following week we changed consultants.

Brendan and myself went to see the consultant. Gillian was our child and we wanted to put up a fight for her. We told him we knew he didn't agree with nebulised antibiotics but we would like to try them. We said we would like a second opinion on the child and would he be able to set up an appointment for us with Dr Denham. He was very nice and immediately went on the phone and got an urgent appointment for the following Monday with Dr Denham. We thanked him very much and as we were leaving he said, "We'll both keep an eye on her but don't expect any miracles with the nebulizer."

By this stage Gillian and myself were becoming closer and closer as each day passed. She was growing into a lovely little girl. The night time physiotherapy became very special for Gillian. Firstly it enabled her to sleep for the night but also it gave her a chance to share time with me, without Brendan and Kelli. This was to become more and more important to her as time went by. She would chat about many different things, ask me lots of questions which I always tried to answer honestly. Looking back I would imagine these night time chats were part of the reason Gillian developed a maturity beyond her years, that and all the time spent in hospital. She still constantly asked about the cure. It was her hope.

Brendan also chatted to her during the early part of the day so she really received an abundance of love and care from both of us. We often spoke about our decision to change doctors and what it had achieved. The G.P. we had changed to was quite blunt and told us that aggressive treatment could prolong Gillian's life for a maximum of five years. He said the clock could not be turned back. The lung damage was there and would progress. If he were right that meant nine years of age at the outside. He said that was with luck on our side and no serious pneumonias. He also said that Kelli should have another sweat test, as she had had a few upper respiratory infections the previous winter. He said there was no point in burying our heads in the sand. We appreciated being told the truth and we believed him regarding Gillian. We knew that the disease was progressive and antibiotics, no matter how strong would only work for so long. Regarding Kelli, Brendan wouldn't hear of another sweat test for her. One negative test was enough for him and she was a big strong bouncer of a child. However, I found the doctor a cold person and the next time I had the flu it was Dr Rita Doyle I phoned to make a house call. Having known her for years I knew she would not take offence and there would be no problem.

Dr Brian Denham pulled off Gillian's vest, and he even looked a little shocked. The skin was falling off her arms. No wonder there had been a problem finding good veins recently. She was virtually wasting away. Every rib was showing. There were big holes under her arms and in the back of her neck. It was upsetting to look at Gillian without clothes on. I always thought, what a pity, whenever I looked at her in the bath. It was hard to comprehend that this was the same child who first came to this hospital two years previously. She now weighed 2st. 2lbs. and looked like a child who was not being fed properly.

Dr Denham spent an hour and a half with us that day, and his registrar and house doctor continued with his clinic. He was very kind and caring and we had felt confident that if anything could be done, he would do it. There was an air of success and confidence about him. He said, "I will change the regime of treatment completely." We were told he would take Gillian in for a month's course of a combination of several very strong IV drugs, "to get the lungs in better shape!" To improve her nutritional status he put her on lots of vitamins, kelovite liquid and pills. Part of the reason why she woke up every night was a sensation in her legs. She called it the "hots" and when she told Dr Denham about it, he immediately recognized the symptoms as vitamin E deficiency.

Dr Brian Denham's greatest immediate achievement for us was his diagnosis of the vitamin E deficiency. From the day he put Gillian on the vitamin E, the "hots" disappeared and by and large she slept right through the night. The four year nightmare of comforting her every night was over. We would often say to each other, "God, if we don't start getting some proper sleep soon, we will never survive." Starting to sleep through the night gave us a chance to re-charge our batteries.

We were happy with this change in treatment, as we at least felt something was being done to try and help the child. Previously we felt like observers at a film, we watched, with no control of the events we were watching. We wanted desperately to fight the disease for Gillian's sake. We would leave no stone unturned.

Dr Denham was worried about Gillian's inability to put on weight. It was a vicious circle. She needed to eat well to be able to fight the chest infections. She had no appetite because of the chronic lung infections. When she did eat well she still didn't put on weight because all her food was going to fight the infection. So, in effect she needed to eat three times the amount of calories a normal child would eat per day to put on weight. All this without an appetite! We realised how impossible and frustrating this whole thing was. It seemed we couldn't win but we couldn't give up either. Now at least we had a doctor who would fight with us.

After the month of October in hospital she seemed in better health. Dr Denham said he would take her into hospital every ten weeks for two weeks, to try and keep her lungs in good shape. He asked us if we would allow him to tube feed her, to try and build up her nutritional status and put on weight. We knew Gillian wouldn't like this on top of needles and drugs through her veins and three hours of banging her every day, but we knew it would help prolong her life so we agreed. This was to happen when she went into hospital in January.

The two children loved Christmas as did Brendan and myself. We always tried to make it very special for them. They would spend weeks writing out lists for Santa. Once Hallowe'en was over their thoughts went straight to the next big event, Christmas. Their minds would be changed many times before the letters finally went off, with exactly the same number of items on each list.

Christmas was very pleasant as usual. My mother cooked a lovely Christmas dinner. I always enjoyed the school holidays as it gave me an opportunity to wind down and get ready for the next term.

At this stage I was still glad I was working, it really was an outlet from the problem and, as Brendan was still working from the house, there was no great pressure on me.

Una, and her husband Dermot, and sons Conall and Gavin came for dinner one evening during the holidays. Gillian had received a lovely electric train on tracks from Brendan's brother in New York. So the four children played for hours with the electric train, with the lights out watching the little red light of the engine chugging around the tracks. We took the girls to see "Cinderella" in the Olympia, which they really enjoyed, except Gillian kept having to go outside to cough.

The New Year 1985 started and Gillian went back into hospital. She had a needle in her arm to take the drugs and a tube down her nose to receive thousands of calories of clini-feed while she slept. Some nights things went smoothly and other nights she would vomit and the tube would come up. They would put it down through her nose again ready to take the liquid food the next night. This went on for three weeks and Gillian put on over half a stone which was a life-line to her. It was a difficult time because between the IV drugs, tube feeding, physiotherapy and nebulized antibiotics, Gillian felt there was little time left for anything else and she began to object to so much treatment. To keep her happy we would take her out of the hospital on a Sunday afternoon to have her tea in the Montrose Hotel. We had taken the children to the Montrose on and off since they were babies. This was our only luxury. We never went on holiday. After tea we would sit in the lobby and relax for a while. Gillian would then have to go back to hospital and we would go home, ready to start another week. One day during the week I would usually go in after school to take Gillian down Grafton Street to McDonalds, to get a break from the hospital. Brendan and myself went in to see her every single night. She would phone and tell us what she wanted us to bring in, hamburger, chips, coke and a list as long as your arm. One could say she was spoilt, but if trying to keep a dying child happy and a bit of weight on was being spoilt, then she was. She was not obviously spoilt, being a very well mannered and polite child, very caring of other people. She worried about the children who she thought were sicker than herself.

Brendan decided early in 1985 he could no longer continue working from the house. He had done so for four years and had pulled Gillian through her early years. His feeling was, no matter what Dr Brian Denham did for Gillian it would only be a matter of a few years before we lost her. He was feeling the strain of the long day and working until late every night. The business could only develop so far because only so many people would come to the house. For him it was time to move out to meet the public. We decided he would look for a shop in the town. However, he agreed he would not take on big overheads for a while so that he could still work flexible hours and help with Gillian. I think he thought that if anything happened to Gillian and he was still working from home he would find it harder to face getting established on the outside.

Gillian was finding it harder to walk up and down the stairs and we were carrying her more and more. We therefore decided we would also move house and buy a house closer to the town with a downstairs toilet. So we began our search for a new house and a shop for Brendan. Had we known what was ahead we would have stayed in our old house and retained surplus cash for what was to come.

Gillian went into Harcourt Street for her IV treatment and tube feeding every few months. She was beginning to feel Harcourt Street was her second home. The staff were very good to her and she knew everyone. Marie Staunton, the play therapist was terrific. She used to call Gillian "Chicken" and she was really lovely to all the children. I felt sorry for the teacher. The children would run off and hide in the linen closet and bathrooms when she would try and entice them to the school room. These were the years of the stringent cutbacks of the eighties.

On one occasion there were nine cystic children in for IV treatment. Gillian told me one evening that the Sister had said to Dr Denham "Dr Denham, we can't cope with all these cystics in for IV at the same time. There are nine of them in this week". "Well, they are not all mine", he replied. "Seven were his patients," laughed Gillian.

The staff of Harcourt Street coped very well under very difficult circumstances. It was a nice cosy, comfortable place with a nice atmosphere for the children. Because it was small it retained its personal touch. Gillian knew all the staff and was especially fond of the porters. They had known her since she was a baby and had laughed and joked with her and the other cystics whom they saw regularly. We all knew the porters, Paddy, James, Alan, John and Leo, the supervisor and they would keep an eye on Kelli in the lobby and ring up to Medical if Kelli needed us. Brendan would go up and down a lot to Kelli and would chat to Paddy and the others. They were very kind and were all very fond of Gillian and thought she and the other cystics were great kids. The porters saw us come and go, in and out, every few months, year in and year out. In the end they watched the children, that they had seen come and go for so long, die. They saw Gillian come down to see Kelli in the lobby with the drip on her arm. They would kiss and hug and two minutes later fight and Gillian perhaps go off up in the lift in a huff.

Five of those nine children have since died from cystic fibrosis in spite of all the efforts of doctors, nurses and parents to keep them alive. They were all great kids who got on with things and never complained about their illness. They all seemed to take it in their stride – the needles, the tubes, the drugs, the physiotherapy, the endless months every year in hospital, the vomiting, coughing and general poor quality of life. They retained their sense of humour throughout everything. Some of the children came from broken marriages. It was very easy to understand how this disease could break a marriage. The daily demands and stress it causes the whole family is quite horrific at times.

We bought a new house in May, just before Gillian's fifth birthday. It had a downstairs toilet and was a five minute walk from the town and my school. However, the move would not take place until 31st October, so we would be just settled in for Christmas. Everyone was looking forward to moving, although the children and ourselves had fond memories of Woodbrook Lawn and we had been very happy there.

In July, Brendan's sister, one year his senior, died in Bradford from Crohn's disease, a bowel disease which she had battled with for years. We waved Brendan off from Dun Laoghaire Pier on a sunny Sunday morning as he headed for England to attend the funeral. We were hardly home when Gillian said, "Is Daddy coming home yet?"

Brendan had never been away from them for even a night so when bedtime came Gillian cried for her Dad. She couldn't understand he would be gone for a few days. Anyone would think he had been gone for a year judging by the excitement when Brendan returned on the following Friday. His sister's death saddened him greatly. A year apart in age they had shared their childhood together. He would mitch and spend the money for the Irish dancing classes and Siobhán would teach him the steps she learned on the way home. He quietly grieved for his sister. She was forty two and left behind a husband, teenage son and daughter.

That summer Gillian once again played out with all the other children. At five, Gillian knew a lot about life. Kelli came in crying one day that summer. I asked her what was wrong and she replied, "Emma said she can't invite me to her party because she would have to invite Gillian and she is always coughing all over the place." That hurt!

After that Gillian would make things clear to new people she met. She would say, "I have cystic fibrosis but you can't catch it from me". At a much later date a child imitated her cough and Gillian said "No Tara, you have it wrong it's like this" and she coughed.

In August Gillian once again returned to Harcourt Street hospital for more IV drugs and tube feeding. On this occasion Dr Denham had obviously decided he was going to attack the Pseudomonas very hard because he knew it was slowly killing Gillian. He kept her in hospital for three long months. I would say he tried every antibiotic and combination of antibiotics available. Every week we would be sure she was coming home only to be told Dr Denham was keeping her a little longer. We worked every day and went into the hospital every night for the three months. At the end of it all, we felt absolutely exhausted and worn out completely, and, as we were also getting ready to move house, Brendan found a little shop for himself. It was a very, very busy time for us.

Finally Dr Denham conceded Gillian could come home. The Pseudomonas was still there! As we were moving house he said she should stay until the move was over. We moved house on Hallowe'en night and we felt bad that Gillian was on her own that night. However, she phoned late to say she had a great time as she had been invited to a party with another child and his family. Gillian always found people to talk to and include her in their activities.

Gillian went back to school in November after her three months in hospital. Although she had only attended three days the previous year, she went into senior infants. This time she went to school every day for seven weeks before catching an infection. She was five, and beautiful, but oh, so thin and fragile. Her teacher was Maureen Walsh who was very understanding of the situation as she had lost a little boy herself some years previously. Maureen later said she was amazed at the effort we would make with the lunch. Breast of chicken, pork chop cut up and wrapped in tin foil, fruit, salad, all sorts of goodies and Gillian would just pick at everything and eat nothing. School took a lot out of Gillian and she would come home absolutely exhausted. She was embarrassed by her cough at first. But within a week in school she could have dropped down dead and the other children would have carried on with their activities without even looking. The racking cough seemed much too strong to come from such a frail body. One would have expected her chest to burst open from the force of the coughing. Gillian could be compared to a young baby. Just as a baby is much stronger than it looks, beneath the frail exterior was a tower of strength of character, courage, determination and will to survive. She wanted to be the same as everyone else, we wanted her to be the same but she wasn't and normality became increasingly difficult.

At first the two children missed our old house and the people in Woodbrook Lawn. They missed the palm tree in our old garden and the stepping stones down through the grass to the little brown shed where their bikes were kept. The new house was nice but we moved on 31st October and the weather was getting very wet, and outside activities were at a standstill for the winter. Hence the children had no opportunity to get to know the local children. Although the new house had four bedrooms they were used to sharing a bedroom and continued to do so for that first year after we moved. They would chat in bed at night and complain bitterly how they missed their old room with Popeye wallpaper. They didn't like the decor of their new room. Little things, as with all children, were important to them.

Brendan opened his shop, "The Dargle Hair Studio" for men on 1st December, just in time for Christmas. It is a nice spacious shop on ground level with good parking opposite and low overheads. However, the shop is situated off the beaten track, away from the mainstream area of Bray. It is situated in Little Bray down over the Dargle River in the old part of the town. Business would depend on his customers going out of their way to come to him. From the day the shop was opened, I immediately felt the pressure.

It didn't open until 10 o'clock each day so that Brendan could still help with the morning shift and he came home for an hour at lunch time to feed Gillian when she wasn't at school. But still he was not free to take her into the hospital and do banking and any other business early in the day. He was happy to be free after tea and didn't mind not working until 10 o'clock at night. It was a welcome and badly needed change for Brendan.

The week the shop opened Gillian went back into hospital once again, with an infection. This was after three months with just a seven week break. It confirmed our fears that Dr Denham would never be able to conquer Pseudomonas. She was home again in time for Christmas, our first in our new house. It had been a hectic year in many ways. Our hope of a cure for cystic fibrosis in time for Gillian had been quietly eroding for some time. We knew it wasn't going to happen. They hadn't yet found the faulty gene or genes, let alone know what was wrong and how or if it could be corrected. This was after thirty years of research.

The new year, 1986, came in with a bang. We awoke one morning to a blanket of white snow everywhere. The Wicklow mountains looked beautiful. Excitement raged through the streets as the children of the area descended on the road to have fun. Gillian joined in with all the others. She was dressed with so many jumpers under her coat that she could hardly bend her arms. Gillian was delighted we allowed her out in the snow with the other children. She thought I would say no when she asked. Her little face lit up with delight when I said she could go out. I knew she wouldn't be able to stay out too long because she would become exhausted and would come in with the satisfaction she had been a part of the excitement. That is exactly what happened. Within half an hour she was back in, clothes changed snuggled up in front of the fire with a hot bowl of soup. She was satisfied. I wondered would she still be with us the next time it snowed? We often went several years without any snow!

The worst year for us since Gillian had been diagnosed, was 1986. The benefits Gillian had derived from Dr Denham's aggressive treatment were beginning to disappear. They had given her a lifeline because he told us later, that when he took her over, there wasn't three months left. So here we were two years later and our pet of the house was still with us and probably would be for another few years. But what did we really have to look forward to? Months in hospital every year, watching her arms being pulled apart looking for veins, tube feeding, hours of physiotherapy, nebulizers and very little energy, and quality of life getting poorer and poorer. They didn't even bother taking x-rays any more because they knew how awful the lungs were. We knew what we were going to face within a few years. It was soul destroying and very frustrating. Living without hope is the most awful state to be in and that was how we lived in 1986.

Brendan and myself had little left to say to each other about the situation we found ourselves in. We had worked hard for Gillian's survival but the cards were stacked against us. Each of us coped in our own way. Brendan preferred not to talk about it too much other than to say that death had a different sting to it than anything else in his experience. He said he just hoped we would be able to pick up the pieces when the inevitable happened. Sometimes he would look at Gillian and shake his head and say, "It's an awful pity."

Brendan had become closer to Gillian than most fathers do with their children because he had been so active in her treatment and had spent so much time with her. He always said the four years he worked from the house and helped look after Gillian would remain with him for ever as a very special time in his life. The memories of her love would keep him going for ever.

Gillian touched Brendan in a very special way and it was sometimes hard to believe, watching them together, that it was the same Brendan I had met back in 1970 in New York. He had worked full time in the lucrative Irish music scene, he, at one stage, flew all around the East Coast and Northern part of America working as a musician – Chicago, Philadelphia, Boston, Cleveland and so on. I never dreamed at that stage he would one day make such a fabulous husband and father. I think he even surprised himself. He was a doting father right from the beginning. I think he must have been one of the first fathers to push a baby in a pram on Bray beach, in 1977, when we first returned from America with Kelli. Having come from America he had no qualms about taking Kelli for a walk on the beach in a pram on his own. My Mum said to him one day,

"Brendan are you taking her out in the pram on your own?"

"Yes, Kay", he replied, "She's my baby and we're off to the beach."

I began to go for walks with Una on a Tuesday evening in the Spring of 1986. It was my first activity on my own without the family since Gillian's diagnosis. Una was great, she would listen while I would verbalise how I would cope when anything happened to Gillian. I was trying to convince myself I would be alright. We would walk on the beach and it was good to get away from the problems for an hour. Sometimes I would be very philosophical about things and other times I would feel so tired I felt I couldn't go on another day, and everything was just too much. Una would always reassure me I was just very tired and would bounce back in a day or two fighting fit to tackle the world. I always did. She said that I always maintained the hardest part was going through the rigorous discipline of the hours and hours of treatment every day for Gillian and knowing it would not make her better, just better for that day and in the end we would still lose her. Now we didn't even have the hope of a breakthrough in the research cystic fibrosis to cling on to. It would be great if they got a breakthrough for all the thousands of other children around the world who had cystic fibrosis, but at this stage we knew Gillian's lungs were beyond being helped by anything. We had nothing to look forward to but the final ultimate downhill course of end-stage lung disease. We were a very happy family, but cystic fibrosis was trying to wreck our lives and all we wanted was to hold onto our beautiful child and see her grow up. We thought of the things other people could take for granted or at least did take for granted even if they shouldn't. At this time the original feeling of sadness and despair we felt back in 1982 kept coming to the fore and became very difficult to suppress.

Una began to drive me into the hospital one evening a week to help ease the pressure on Brendan who was working hard to try and build up the business. For the first time Una began to get a real insight into cystic fibrosis. There would usually be several of the cystics in for treatment with Gillian. She saw them all going around with their cannulas in their arms or their nebulizers, coughing, vomiting, laughing and joking. She saw it all. For the first time she saw me banging the back off Gillian, doing physiotherapy. She just looked as I started the pounding and Gillian almost immediately started coughing and bringing up the phlegm. Una couldn't watch this, it upset her and she took a walk into another ward. It was another world to her as she had two lovely healthy boys close in age to our two. She once said everyone should spend a week in a children's hospital and they would never again moan about trivial things.

My Mum and Dad stayed with Gillian during the day at this time and were a great support and help to us. Without my parents and Una, we would never have managed. Kelli stayed sometimes with my parents and other times with Una when we went back and forth to the hospital. Other times she came in and waited patiently in the lobby.

Our day started at 7.00 a.m. and we both worked and looked after Gillian until late. It was very difficult but we did our utmost to keep the two children as happy as possible, mainly by our love. Every time Gillian went to school she picked up a cold or bug or infection, so she didn't go much. Because she was home so much she just loved the family outings on Sunday for tea in the Montrose. We threw caution to the wind, overindulged her and overspent, and didn't worry about the future. The present became all important.

As time went by, Brendan's departure from working at home took its toll on me. By the time the summer holidays came I was very tired. It was an emotional tiredness more than anything else, brought on by the realisation that all avenues had been explored for Gillian and time was running out, barring a miracle. We were determined to have a lovely summer and we did. The long sunny days in Ireland are beautiful. Even if it rains early in the day the sun always seems to emerge by late afternoon into early evening. I've always found this one of the joys of living here. The sun shining over Bray Head and Killiney Hill and Howth on a summer's evening is sheer bliss and something which always remained in my memory when I was away in America, Portugal and London. Living by the sea has many advantages that people in Ireland take for granted. We all love the sea and I don't think I would ever like to live far from it again. In fact, I find a certain peace and security in Ireland I never found anywhere else. I suppose one has to go away to come back and the return is all the sweeter. I laughed once when Pat Staunton, Brendan's wise old father came out to visit us in New York in 1975. He had lived in the same town in Westchester County fifty years previously and had returned to inherit the farm in Galway. He looked across at the Long Island Sound from New Rochelle, which was beautiful and he said, "I never settled here myself, Veronica and I was glad to go back. It's always had that foreign appearance!"

We made the most of the days Brendan was free, Sunday and Monday. We had picnics in Brittas Bay and the Waterfall, walks in Killiney and Dalkey and Sunday tea in the Montrose. The rest of the week I spent a lot of time on Bray beach with the two children. Gillian would push herself beyond what she was able to do and pay the price afterwards. I remember one sunny Monday in Brittas Bay she tried to keep up with Kelli rolling down the sand dunes. Her laughter rang around the sparsely populated beach. I kept saying, "Take it easy Gill."

She wouldn't listen and eventually flopped down exhausted. We rushed back to Bray with Gillian conked out in the back of the car. She lay on the couch for three days trying to get her strength back. Then she was back in action ready for more excitement and fun.

In the second week of August Gillian returned to Harcourt Street hospital for more treatment. The weather was very hot and it was a pity Gillian had to be cooped up in hospital. We took her to Stephen's Green and McDonalds as much as possible. Some days I would go in and bring her home after her second dose of drugs at 2 o'clock and have her back at 11 o'clock for the third dose.

Brendan had settled into his new shop well and was happy he had made the move. As he said, "There is a time for everything."

Quite unexpectedly "Hurricane Charlie" swept through Bray. The Dargle River broke its banks and "The Dargle Hair Studio" was submerged below five feet of dirty, filthy, muddy water from the river. It happened on a Monday night. Tuesday morning we waded through a foot of water into the shop. As we opened the door in the hall of the shop, death certificates and wreaths of flowers floated in front of us from the funeral parlour next door. Proceeding into our shop we saw the water mark an inch below the light switch and still a foot of water remained. Everything was destroyed, towels, tables, mirrors, dryers, magazines, brushes swept from one end of the room to the other. It was soul destroying, we had worked so hard to do up the shop just eight months previously. Hundreds of pounds of new lino and new dryers were destroyed. We had no insurance because the premium the insurance companies wanted was much too expensive. The Dargle River had not flooded in thirty years and the first year we were there it happened, such was our luck. While everyone else was looking in amazement at the damage and destruction we began hosing out our shop while there was still good water pressure. My Mum helped us and by twelve o'clock Tuesday night we were well on the road to recovery. It set us back financially but after what we had already gone through with Gillian it was minor. We pressed on as usual and the shop re-opened for business on the Friday. It was bad luck, but when we looked at the people of Little Bray whose homes had been destroyed, we considered ourselves lucky. People were months trying to get their lives back in order. Homes and belongings were ruined. The smell of stagnant water remained in the area for months. We considered ourselves lucky to have a comfortable home in another part of Bray to return to at night.

Gillian came home from another hospitalisation in time to return to school in September 1986. She would repeat senior infants with Maureen Walsh as she had only attended for seven weeks the previous year. By this stage Maureen said she truly looked very fragile but within that fragile body a strength and maturity of mind and spirit existed way beyond her years. When a child in the class would do something silly Gillian would make eye contact with Maureen as if to say "Silly thing".

She was still amazed at the effort we made with the lunch and not surprised that Gillian was even making a more feeble attempt at eating it. She saw a deterioration in Gillian since the previous September.

Although Gillian was repeating senior infants it was decided she would make her first Holy Communion the following May, just before her seventh birthday. We were hoping she would be able to attend school as much as possible, still grasping at the idea of keeping things normal! We were being silly really because there was nothing normal about our life as other people with healthy children know 'normal'. I suppose we didn't really realise how abnormal it all was to outsiders.

I remember a friend of mine, Margaret Flood who works for Aer Lingus, used to come out to dinner once or twice a year. I would have Gillian's second treatment done before she came and would do the third physiotherapy, nebulizer and drugs after she had left. Apart from Gillian having the odd coughing fit and looking a little thinner each time she came, she didn't realise how much input there was into Gill. However, on one occasion she decided she would stay the night. It was a Friday afternoon when Margaret arrived. I had to leave her watching television to do Gillian's treatment. We had a nice evening meal and on this occasion Gillian ate very little and had to be constantly encouraged to eat. After dinner Margaret and myself spent the evening chatting and catching up the year's news. Margaret, being single with a very good job usually travelled extensively every year, so she would tell me all about her travels. Later in the evening I went off once again to look after Gillian and settle her for the night. Margaret heard Gillian coughing during the night and while she was resting the following morning, heard Gillian coughing and later having her first physiotherapy and nebulizer treatment for the day. Before Margaret left later on Saturday morning to go off golfing she said to me, "Veronica, I never really realised how much of your time it takes to look after Gillian. My goodness, the child takes all of your time. I know you've said in the past you've very little time for anything else after teaching and looking after her, but until I actually saw you in action with her, it didn't really sink in. It's a dreadful disease, isn't it. How do you keep going with it year after year?"

"I know it takes all of our spare time Margaret, but that does not bother us. We would gladly do it for ever for Gillian. It's a little soul-destroying to know deep down we are still going to lose her in the end. But at least we know we did our very best, and we will keep doing it as long as we are lucky enough to have her."

"Does Gillian not mind all that physiotherapy, banging her lungs for hours every day?"

"No, because she feels so much better after it and she can continue breathing for another few hours, she doesn't remember when it didn't happen to her, it's part of her life in the same way Harcourt Street Hospital and all the needles and tube feeding is. She never complains."

"I really didn't understand until today what you all go through because you always play it down in your conversation. You always have a good laugh when I come out. It doesn't seem to get you or Brendan down", commented Margaret.

This was the first time we had really spoken in detail about Gillian's illness and that was only because Margaret had been affected by what she had seen. She went off in her new white Honda Civic to her golfing with plenty to think about regarding cystic fibrosis.

# 5. Seeds are Sown

In late October 1986 Gillian became very ill. It started with a stomach virus. We nursed her at home day and night for a week. When we took her into Dr Denham he said he would have to admit her as her lungs were filling up. This was his polite way of saying she had pneumonia! We had been doing physiotherapy five times a day for the previous three days.

Every few hours she was getting choked up and the physiotherapy was the only way of giving her relief. It was touch and go for a few days. Gillian just lay lifeless in the bed and we waited once more for her to respond to the IV antibiotics. During these first few days a house doctor told me that in other Dublin hospitals Gillian would have already been wound down. I knew this was true. It was Dr Denham's devotion to the badly affected children and input into them that kept them going for the few extra years. After a few days Gillian began to smile at us once again and we knew she was on the mend. However, it took her a long time to bounce back. She came home from hospital after three weeks. She lay on the couch for a month and hardly ever moved off it, before going back to hospital again for more IV. During the month lying on the couch at home I would chat and cuddle Gillian late at night after the physiotherapy. One particular evening she looked me straight in the eyes and said, "Mum, I want you to promise me that if anything happens to me, you won't be sad. I want you to get on with your life with Dad and Kelli and enjoy it, won't you do that for me?"

I was shocked and surprised. These words remember, were coming from a beautiful child of six and a half years. I knew then how ill Gillian really was. We kissed each other and we both cried together.

"Gillian, do you really feel that bad?" I asked.
"Mum, I'm just oh so very tired all the time. I can't do anything."
"Listen Gill, you will pick up again in time, you always do. You have to hang in there and keep warm, eat well, rest and we will nurse and therapy you back to health."
"You're a great Mum and Dad and I love you all very much. You're the best in the world and I'm very lucky to have you all," she replied.
"If you promise to keep fighting cystic fibrosis, I promise if we lose the battle I will try not to be too sad and get on with my life, okay," I continued. She promised and we laughed and hugged.
I didn't tell Brendan about this conversation because I knew it would upset him and make him sad. It made me realise that Gillian was losing the hope of a cure being found. Talk like this from a six year old told me really how Gillian felt. She went in and out of hospital that whole winter and lay on the couch in-between. We did the treatment every day, talked to her a lot and kept her comfortable. People would ask me "How's Gillian, Veronica?" and I would reply, "Fine thanks."
We began to almost accept Gillian lying on the couch every day as being fine. She watched television, ate very little, had her treatment and chatted when she had the energy. She smiled when we said something funny. Sometimes her friend Claire would come in and they would sit and play a game for a while but Gillian would tire easily and soon go back to the couch.
She was there every day when I came in from school. I would immediately hug her and have a chat and a cup of coffee before doing her physiotherapy. She didn't seem to get any worse or any better. It's amazing what one can get used to. I wondered would she ever run or play on the street again! I didn't think so.
Late at night when everyone was in bed I would sometimes sit and think. I had read Margaret Mc Stay's book *Colin* and I would sit

and look at the picture of Colin's lovely little face on the cover of the book, and think how great it was his life had been saved by a liver transplant. I looked at Colin night after night and re-read parts of Margaret's book, and slowly I began to think. If Colin could get a new liver, why couldn't Gillian get new lungs? It remained a vague thought for a long time but nevertheless the thought was planted in my subconscious. I said nothing to anyone. Christmas came and went. It was pleasant and quiet and we thought it was possibly Gillian's last. She went back into hospital in mid-January and returned at the beginning of February. The sun started to shine as spring approached and our Gillian seemed a little better. She was like a little squirrel hibernating for the winter. With spring she began to move off the couch and become a little more active again. She would put on her coat and go for short walks up and down, outside the house. Gradually she improved.

After Christmas I had read an article about someone in England having a heart and lung transplant because they had a lung disease. It said although their heart was alright it was easier to transplant the heart and lungs together. This article interested me very much, and the thoughts I had when I looked at "Colin" returned. If a heart and lung transplant could save Gillian's life why couldn't we try and get one for her. I knew in my heart that what I was looking for was a miracle. There were thousands of cystics in Ireland and England and they certainly couldn't all have transplants. I kept saying to myself, "Don't be silly, accept the reality that Gillian will die".

In spring I began my walks again with Una every Tuesday evening, for an hour after everything was done at home. I usually picked Una up at 9 o'clock and we would have a walk and a chat usually with me doing most of the talking. On this particular night we were sitting in the car outside Una's house. I said, "I would like to try and put Gillian forward for a heart and lung transplant. I don't know if I have the energy for what it would involve. Where would we get the money, how would we go to England and hold down jobs and would the English authorities give it to a child outside their country when they have so many of their own cystic fibrosis children? After all that, would it work and would Gillian be up to it?"

Una looked at me and said, "You'll do it if it's in your mind." But she did agree it would be a big thing to even attempt.

I put it to the back of my mind because I was so busy teaching and looking after Gillian, doing the therapy three times a day and keeping food in her. There was little time for thinking too deeply about anything. Also, I had mentioned to Brendan that there had been a few heart and lung transplants done in England and what about trying to get one for Gillian. I think he thought I was a bit mad. At that time he couldn't imagine someone going around with someone else's heart and lungs. I reminded him about Colin McStay, the little baby from Dublin, who had been transplanted with a new liver in America two years previously.

Anyway, he didn't really give me much encouragement and I suppose he thought I would forget about it.

Two months passed and then Gillian was back in Harcourt Street once again for IV treatment with yet another infection. I hadn't thought any more about transplants. In the meantime I had heard about a new oral drug for Pseudomonas called Ciprofloxacin.

I was in the treatment room on the Medical Ward one evening with Gillian waiting for her to get her IV treatment. Gillian was thin and pale and sick. I said to the sister who was doing the drugs, "Do you think Gillian could be helped with the new oral drug Ciprofloxacin?"

Her reply was, "How could any oral drug help Gillian when she is getting very little benefit any more from strong IV drugs?"

I knew this meant we were really running out of time so I said, "What about a heart and lung transplant?"
She said, "Have you been offered a transplant? You know they are very expensive".
I just looked at her and said, "No, I haven't been offered one but I'll certainly look for one and I don't care how expensive they are."
This was only the first of many incidents where money was to be the centre of the conversation.
The seed was further sown in my mind that I might pursue a transplant for Gillian. I got hope from the sister's comment. She made it sound possible if one had money. The following Monday afternoon Brendan and myself met Dr Denham and a young house doctor at the top of the stairs outside the Medical ward. We discussed Gillian for a few minutes and then I suddenly said to him casually, "Dr Denham, do you think Gillian could benefit from a heart and lung transplant?" He seemed quite surprised by the question but replied that it would be a lot to put a young child through with no guarantee of success, and the longest survivor in the world of such an operation was only five years. I replied that five years was a long time if it's your child. The conversation was quite casual, and it concluded by Dr Denham saying he supposed there would be no harm in opening up communications with Papworth, if we wished. He indicated he regarded it as pie in the sky. That was in April 1987. After that we were busy getting ready for Gillian's First Holy Communion and I didn't think about it for another while. I just think that every time I thought about a transplant, I became emotionally exhausted and did not have the strength or will to do anything about it. I had been offered nothing, it was being left entirely to ourselves to pursue if we had the will. At that stage I really didn't even have Brendan on my side. I didn't think at that point I would take the matter any further. Too many factors seemed to be against it.

She looked beautiful on her Communion day in her lovely white dress and long dark hair, but she didn't look well. It crossed my mind we might bury her in that very dress. She seemed to be forcing herself to be active, yet only we ourselves saw the effort she had to make at times. We had seen her like this many times before but she always bounced back and went on to have better spells afterwards. We hoped she would improve. Two weeks later we went off to Lourdes for four days.

The group included a priest and a few people from a local parish church, a group from Gorey, Co. Wexford and some people from the Northside of Dublin. It was an adult group and a lovely atmosphere prevailed among them.

We arrived late at night and I discovered when I went to give Gillian her nebulizer treatment, that the adapter I had brought for the nebulizer was square and the plug in the wall was round. It wouldn't matter for once I said to myself, did the physiotherapy and Gillian and myself prepared for bed. It was twelve o'clock when we put the lights out. Shortly afterwards Gillian began to cough. She continued coughing for a long time. Finally at about two o'clock I turned the light on and gave her a drink. Instinct told me that without the Ventolin through the nebulizer we would get no sleep that night. In the end I went down to the front desk of the hotel with the adaptor for the nebulizer and explained my plight to the chap on the desk. He was extremely nice and within five minutes, Gillian was on her nebulizer plugged into a French adaptor. After that we went off to sleep.

The realisation that Gillian was on the down stretch was evident in so many ways. She couldn't miss the nebulized antibiotics and strong dose of Ventolin for even one night. Imagine trying to skip a physiotherapy! The people in the next room must have heard Gillian coughing. Betty and her friend from Gorey knocked on my door in the morning and asked if I needed anything. They were lovely, very kind. "If you could just bring us up some coffee and toast please, it would help". If we were to be ready to go to Mass we would have to get moving with the nebulizer and physiotherapy. Gillian was very tired but we were ready to go to Mass with the group.

It was Gillian's seventh birthday and she wore her Communion dress to church that morning. I pushed her along to church in a push chair . The priest from Gorey, Father Matt Kelly was very outgoing and Gillian and himself became friendly. Someone told him it was Gillian's birthday and at the end of the Mass he sang "Happy Birthday" to her. It was a small cosy church and it was emotional for me to see the Irish group singing to Gillian. Her long shining dark hair fell down over the white dress and her brown eyes sparkled. Only the dark rings under her eyes and her sinking jaws betrayed her illness.

We enjoyed the few days in Lourdes. Everyone made a big fuss of Gillian. I felt an immense amount of goodwill on that trip, with that particular group of Irish people. They were strangers and yet they seemed to realise how difficult things were for us and were extremely kind. Gillian coughed a lot, and although I took no notice after all the years, other people I'm sure found it stressful to listen to. I'm sure they knew she didn't have good lungs. She needed physiotherapy four times a day on that trip.

We went to Mass each morning with the group and Gillian loved the atmosphere at the nightly candle-light processions. I would push her around in the push chair and she would hold her candle and smile and enjoy listening to the thousands of people from all over the world singing the Ave Marie and other hymns. After the nightly procession, people from the group would sit around in the hotel lobby and have a drink and chat for a while. It was nice and relaxing.

Gillian and myself went into the baths on the second day. Later I asked her if she wanted to go back again to the baths. "No," she replied, "She knows I would like to get better, to go again would be begging, once is enough".

Gillian and myself rested every afternoon so that we would be able to go out to the procession at night. Once again, during one of our long chats regarding life and death and what it was all about, Gillian said if anything happened to her she wanted me to get on with life and not to be sad about her. This was the second time she had said this in less than a year.

"I don't think they will get the cure for cystic fibrosis in time for me Mum, will they?".

To be without hope is the most devastating feeling in the world and I didn't want our little girl to ever be without some sort of hope. Brendan and myself had always wanted her to know the truth and to accept she had a serious illness which had to be fought tooth and nail. She knew we had already changed doctors to fight the disease and she had confidence that if anything further could be done we would do it. When a child on the street said to her one day when she was six, "You're going to die", Gillian was able to look at the child and reply, "Everyone is going to die and no one knows when."

We were very proud of the way we had trained her, because no one could ever shock or hurt her because we had it all so well explained since she was very young. Brendan was always telling her she had absolutely nothing ever to worry about, that she would be looked after and loved everyday and moment of her life and she would never be sad.

So on this occasion in Lourdes I replied, "Gillian, they could get a cure for cystic fibrosis anytime. We just have to enjoy each day and not worry too much about your disease. They are also coming out with new treatment and new drugs all the time. Life is changing constantly and nothing ever stays the same. Nothing is going to happen to you because we will keep fighting the disease together and you will go on for years."

I gave her a big hug and she was happy. I was worried because she only really spoke like this when she didn't feel well and got nervous about herself. Normally all her conversations were enquiring about life in general. She loved to chat and discuss all sorts of things, life and living always intrigued her.

On the night before we left Lourdes we returned from the night procession for the last time. I sat in the lobby of the hotel for a while chatting to different people we had met. Someone took Gillian off to buy her a drink. As she walked back across the lobby towards me with a bottle of coke in her hand and a smile on her face the thought of a transplant flashed through my mind for the first time in a few months. I think I knew that night I would look for a heart and lung transplant for Gillian. I knew that no Irish cystic had received one. I knew there were 800 cystics in the Republic and I didn't think anyone was likely to shout "Come on cystics, let's send you all to England to get new hearts and lungs, at a cost of maybe £50,000 to £60,000."

Instinct told me my deep love for Gillian would lead me down a very difficult, stressful, frustrating, nerve-racking road to possibly nowhere. Deep inside myself I knew it might be more than I could handle. Would I have the inner strength and stamina for what might lie ahead? It would have been much easier to accept, like everyone else in Ireland who had a cystic child, that when the lungs ran out of tissue, the child died! But I couldn't accept it easily.

On the return flight home the next evening Gillian said she had really enjoyed the few days away. She asked me what I thought about miracles. I replied that it depended what she meant by a miracle. I told her anything was possible but I had never seen any physical miracles.

"Do you think you will be cured Gill?" I asked. She replied, "No, but I think that I will be much better than before."
My wheels were turning as to how I would go about looking for a transplant but I didn't tell her. I told Gillian there was something about Lourdes that I liked very much. To be honest we would probably never have gone there if she had been healthy. I felt a certain peace inside the grotto area and for the first time, an acceptance for whatever was to be. I knew from that day on, I wouldn't worry about what couldn't be changed, but would fight for what might be possible to the bitter end.

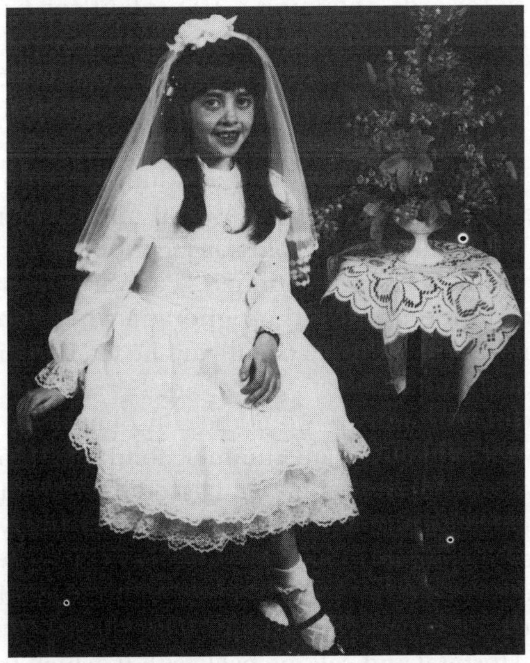

*Communion day (May 1987)*

# 6. New Beginning, New Hope

Excitement stirred in my veins at the thought that maybe there could be new hope that Gillian could live longer. I felt that I would take it one step at a time, in the same way that we had taken our life one day at a time. In the summer of 1987, as I began my journey towards obtaining a transplant for Gillian I had no idea how far it would be possible to get towards achieving my goal. "Pie in the sky". "A long shot". "Experimental surgery". "An awful lot of money". All these things rang in my ears. I don't think I even knew, at that stage, whether or not cystics were suitable candidates. I just knew that heart and lung transplants were being performed in England. The hospital and doctor I had heard about were Harefield and Professor Jacoub, the Egyptian surgeon. When Dr Denham had mentioned "Papworth Hospital", I didn't want to sound too interested or ignorant, so I hadn't gone into it too much, just kept the name in my head. I didn't have a clue where Papworth was.

I felt, knowing I had tried, would be consoling even if I failed.

Within a week of starting my summer holidays I phoned the Cystic Fibrosis Association in Dublin, and asked if they could give me any information about heart and lung transplants. They were not able to tell me anything about them. I got the impression from the tone of the girl's voice that I was odd to be even asking about such things. However, they did say they would find out the address of Papworth Hospital and call me back with it, which they duly did.

Before I wrote to Papworth I decided to phone the Cystic Fibrosis Organisation in London, because I was very anxious to know what was happening in the cystic fibrosis world. I felt a little disillusioned, and thought because the cystic fibrosis office in Dublin knew nothing, that maybe cystics were just not considered suitable candidates for transplantation. If that was the case and no surgeon would transplant a cystic, I was wasting my time. Surely, I said to myself the organisation in Dublin would have had up to date information.

I phoned the Cystic Fibrosis Trust in London one Tuesday afternoon in the third week of July. To my delight I encountered a lovely gentleman called Damian Roberts, who was sweet music to my ears. He spent one and a half hours speaking to me on the phone and gave me all the information I needed. He also made me feel he cared and would support me in any way he could.

I told him all about Gillian, and the fact that we had been told three years previously she wouldn't live more than five years, at the most. Also, we were noticing ourselves the gradual deterioration and had no reason to believe the doctors were wrong. "Can you give me any information about heart and lung transplants? Could a cystic child get one?" I asked.

"Yes Veronica", he replied. "You are certainly on the right track. They have been doing heart and lung transplants on young cystic fibrosis adults in Papworth Hospital in Cambridge for about two years now. They started in October 1985, and although it is still considered "experimental surgery", the results and survival rates are quite promising."

"Does the cystic fibrosis come back in the new lungs?" I asked.

"No, not so far, they just didn't know whether it would or not and were very reluctant to do cystics for that reason. But Mr John Wallwork, the heart and lung surgeon at Papworth, felt cystics should get a chance because they were such fighters, such determined and fabulous people. He felt if the genetic factors didn't come back they could be one of the biggest groups to benefit from transplants in the future. Damian had all the time in the world to speak to me. I didn't even think of the huge phone bill. It was so nice to be able to communicate with someone up to date with twentieth century developments in modern medicine, and happy to give of their time, I didn't feel I was bothering him. He pointed out that it was only carried out as a last resort when all conventional medicines had failed and there was absolutely nothing to lose. He didn't think any children had been transplanted to date, but said it would be the next step, he was sure.

Damian told me about a Dr Littlewood in Manchester, who he said was an excellent cystic doctor and would be very good for doing a general assessment on the stage Gillian was at, if we weren't sure. I just said I'd think about it. I gathered that in Britain many cystics went to local hospitals rather than special cystic units. We were already attending the National Children's Hospital and were quite happy with Dr Denham's handling of the disease. We knew he would be able to furnish an accurate report of Gillian's stage of the disease if and when it was required.

I explained the exact regime of treatment Dr Denham had Gillian on, the intensive, regular, very expensive strong IV drugs, nebulized antibiotics and Ventolin, complete vitamin supplements, Vitamin E, Creon pancreatic capsules used to break down fats and of course, intensive daily physiotherapy., Damian agreed it seemed to be the latest aggressive treatment and sounded as if there was no more to be done other than what was already being done. Damian concluded the conversation by saying he would put me on their cystic fibrosis mailing list and he would send me all the up to date information on heart and lung transplants, survival rate and the possible complications. He also asked me to let him know how things went with Gillian and said to give him a ring any time I needed to know anything.

Once I knew that British cystics were already getting transplants, I knew nothing would stop me pursuing one for Gillian. I felt very happy and hopeful after my conversation with Damian Roberts. I told Brendan and he said, "What makes you think a hospital in Britain will give an Irish child a transplant – they must have plenty of their own cystics? Anyway Veronica, even if they did who would pay for it? We are already up to our eyes in debt to the banks after five years of cystic fibrosis and Harcourt Street Hospital. Personally I think you are dreaming and it will only bring more disappointment to you when it doesn't work."

"Well, I'm going to try, and if they can't do it here then the Irish Government should pay for it." This is how I felt and I sat down the next day and wrote my first letter to Papworth Hospital.

I received a reply to my letter within ten days. It was a very nice letter from one of the Papworth team, Dr Higgenbottom. He said they were indeed considering cystic fibrosis patients with end-stage lung disease for transplant. So far they hadn't transplanted anyone under 10 years but hoped to begin a programme in conjunction with Great Ormond Street Childrens' Hospital in the near future. He asked me to get Dr Denham to send him on a report of his findings of Gillian's condition. I immediately sent a copy of the letter to Dr Denham and asked him to send the report. Hearing nothing from Dr Denham, I presumed he had sent the report and I waited patiently.

Amazingly Gillian's health seemed to improve that summer and although she still tired very easily she seemed better than she had been for quite some time. She had finally recovered from the bad infection the previous winter. We enjoyed the temporary remission as it were, and once again had a nice summer in between my phone calls and letters to London. We did all the usual things we did every summer and were very surprised that Gillian was as well as she was. She seemed to have new fight in her and was more determined than ever to survive. To our mind she grew more beautiful in herself, kind, gentle and loving by the day, although she didn't look very well. At seven she could converse with the maturity of a teenager. She was beginning to be a most interesting little girl to be around.

Kelli and herself communicated very well most of the time and were good company for each other despite the three year chronological age difference. Of course, there was the usual fighting and jealousy that exists between sisters. That made us feel quite normal at times.

During that summer of 1987 she heard me on the phone to Damian Roberts in London and saw me writing letters. She asked what it was all about. I told her I was finding out about heart and lung transplants in England to see if we would be able to get her one some day. She replied, "I don't want a heart and lung transplant. I want to keep my own heart and lungs."

"Yes, but when your own lungs get much worse they won't be any good to you Gill and you might be glad to get new ones. I'm only finding out about it." We talked about it gradually as I proceeded with the negotiations and I told her what I knew as we went along. I also told her it wasn't something you ran off to England to look for at the last minute. It had to be planned and arranged. Gillian really wasn't that interested at the beginning. I explained how great it would be if she ever got the chance to get new lungs and all the things she would be able to do with them.

At the beginning of September, I phoned Margaret McStay for the first time. Having read the book several times and now having taken steps myself in the same direction she had taken, I decided it would be nice to speak to her. Margaret was very nice when I explained my position. She told me they were off to America the very next day and she would give me a ring when she returned a month later. She also said she would find out what was happening in the States with cystics and heart and lung transplants. Margaret McStay was a stranger to me that day in September 1987 but she was very supportive from our first conversation and I knew she understood what I was going through.

A week later, I received a phone call from Marian Gavin who said Margaret McStay had told her about me. She was ringing me because her son Jamie had received a heart and lung transplant two years previously. He had been the world's youngest and Ireland's first. Jamie didn't have cystic fibrosis but Marian gave me great hope. So here we were with two new people in our lives who had been successfully down the road we were hoping to embark on. This bit of support at this time was really lovely and much appreciated. I had many questions for both Margaret and Marian in the years that followed and they were always most helpful and kind in different ways.

Gillian was due to see Dr Denham in early October and I knew he would probably have heard from Papworth. The day I was seeing him in the clinic we were going over to the Royal Academy of Music afterwards, for Kelli to audition to learn the flute with an excellent well-known flute teacher, who had taught James Galway at one time, Mrs Doris Keogh. Kelli was very anxious and determined to pass the audition and learn with Mrs Keogh as she was going to be "a famous flautist". At ten Kelli didn't understand the implications of her innocent statement.

We were all uptight as we set off for Dublin. Kelli worried about her first audition and Gillian worried that Dr Denham would say she had to go into hospital once again for treatment. I was anxious to know what Papworth had to say.

Dr Denham seemed a little edgy. The nurse took Gillian off to be weighed and he told me he had a letter from Papworth Hospital. They had put Gillian on their waiting list for assessment for heart and lung transplantation. I was delighted and obviously showed my delight which he didn't really share.

He said, "You know I don't really agree with transplants". I asked him why and he replied, "You could lose her on the table you know".

"We are going to lose her anyway, aren't we Dr Denham?" I responded.

"Yes", was the reply. "How long?" I asked. "Two years, maybe a little longer".

"So we will go down fighting and maybe win, we have nothing to lose," I told him.

He concluded, "Well, as long as that's your attitude, but remember, this is just step one and still a long way from a transplant".

We rushed off to the Academy for Kelli's audition in great spirits. Kelli calmed down when she saw another girl coming out of the audition crying and saying, "Why on earth are they wasting time auditioning if they have no places?" Kelli played beautifully and although they had no places, Mrs Keogh said she would accept Kelli but we would have to wait a few months until she sorted out a time. She told her she was taking her out of two hundred applications. I've never seen Kelli so delighted as that day. She kept saying, "I'm going to learn the flute with the best teacher in Ireland."

When we arrived back in Bray the two girls rushed into their father's Hair Studio. "Dad, Doris Keogh has accepted me out of two hundred children", and, "Dad, I'm on the waiting list to be assessed for the transplant". We all went off for a Pizza that evening instead of cooking. Brendan and myself smiled as we looked at the two happy little faces in front of us, each having received important news that day.

Gillian went into hospital for her IV treatment the following week. She had not been in hospital for five months! This was one of the longest breaks we had experienced.

"I told you I'd be much better after Lourdes," she chirped.
The following Friday I went straight into the hospital after school to see Gillian. Brendan's brother, Michael, a farmer from Galway was coming to Dublin for the week-end and he was staying with us so I'd arranged to meet him in the hospital at 5 p.m. The doors of the ward swung open and Michael appeared with a football bag in each hand. A typical bachelor, he had only himself and his good time to worry about. Battling through the rush hour traffic en-route to Bray I told Michael we were putting Gillian forward for a heart and lung transplant. He replied, "those things are very expensive, sure she'll be happy in heaven." I was stunned and was about to stop the car and tell him to get out when I thought of Brendan's eighty-eight year old father Pat in Galway. Pat wouldn't like any trouble. I looked at him and replied, "Yes, well she'll be happy here if we have any say in it, never mind about heaven".
I don't think he even realised how outrageous he was. I thought to myself the same fellow has probably spent the price of several transplants on pints of porter over the past twenty-five years, no trouble to him. Brendan just said not to take any notice of Michael. At least Michael was honest. I think many people felt the same but never had the nerve to say so. They say money is not everything but we found out, after one's health, it is everything! It even controls life and death. We had never put much value on it up to this point in our life. We always had enough so didn't need to think about it. But through the experience of Gillian's sickness I realised I had been naive and was to learn that money is very important to most people and will be important to me in future.
The following week was very sad. One of the children we had met on and off over the years was in the next bed to Gillian. He was very sick and for the first time I knew we were watching a child dying from cystic fibrosis. David was about twelve or thirteen. I had seen photos of his confirmation earlier that year up on the

board in the corridor. Every breath he took was horrific for him. He looked as if he was in agony trying to breathe and each time he took a breath his heart could be visibly seen moving up and down in his chest. I knew this was the final stage of the disease. I never wanted to watch my child go through it. There seemed little the staff could do for him. He was a lovely gentle child and I had seen him lively and well six months previously. The oxygen seemed to give some relief.

On the Friday afternoon Gillian was getting dressed to go home so she had the curtain pulled around her bed. A gentleman was visiting David and he said to him, "I've brought you a game David to play with your friends". "I've no friends", was the depressed reply. "I'm your friend", chirped Gillian from the other side of the curtain. David managed a little laugh before going into another coughing fit and vomiting. We said goodbye five minutes later and I knew there was death on his face. He died two days later and I was glad Gillian wasn't in the hospital to witness it. We knew eight or nine other cystics quite well and David was only the first of five to be lost to the awful disease in the next few years. We didn't tell Gillian that David had died and she presumed he got better because she could often go a year or so without meeting up with someone. She had been very sick herself on occasions and had seen some of the others very sick many times and they had always bounced back. People always expected cystics to bounce back but the time always comes when some of them don't! It was over a year later she asked and we told her about David.

I was very quiet in the car that Friday evening driving home and Gillian knew there was something wrong. "Mum, aren't you glad I'm coming home again, you're very quiet and it's not like you. What's wrong?" "Just tired Gill, working all week and in and out of the hospital." That was true but I was also thinking of the young boy we had just left.

I spoke to Damian Roberts in the Cystic Fibrosis office in London again and told him Gillian was on the list for the assessment. He was pleased for us. I asked him to get me some information about costing for the assessment and a transplant. He mentioned an E.112 form, the scheme whereby treatment not available in one's own country but available in another E.C. Country enabled you to get that treatment, and your Government pays the Government of the country where you receive the treatment.

He said he would try and find out the cost of the assessment and a transplant. I told him we were broke after all the years of heating the house twenty-four hours a day, going back and forth to hospital each day, for several months every year and bringing all sorts of goodies every time.

A few weeks later I asked Dr Denham if I should apply for the E.112. He said, "I doubt you will be able to get that in the present economic climate".

"Well, why should any Irish child be deprived of life-saving treatment which is available to English children? If our Government can't provide this treatment they will have to pay for us to go out of the country for it."

"Well, you will have to tell them that."

"I will," I replied.

I did nothing for a while and thought carefully about the whole thing.

# 7. *Financial Problems*

I knew that if the Irish Government would not pay for a transplant for Gillian then I would not hesitate to go public, to appeal to the Irish people. I would not ask anyone on the face of this earth for anything for myself, but for Gillian's life, money would not stop me. However, we didn't even know if Gillian would be a suitable candidate for a transplant yet!

Should we go ahead and wait until after the assessment to approach them? Then we would know more.

Brendan kept saying, "Why not try and get the assessment over and see if Gillian is accepted for a transplant before approaching the Government to pay for it. We don't know yet if we'll need them at all. Let's get through step one. You've been told it's a can of worms, so tread carefully."

Cystics in the U.K. had been having transplants for two years at this stage, so someone here was bound to look for it for their child or themselves. I couldn't see why it was or could be considered a can of worms. While there were 800 cystics in the country, these would all be at various stages of the disease. Some would not be suitable for transplantation, some would just not want a transplant and many would not need one. Some might need it but not know they did, and so on. As Dr Denham said a few years later in the *Irish Medical Times* calling for the setting up of a cystic fibrosis Transplant Project, "The demand for cystic transplants, if a programme were started here, would be about ten a year."

However, I suppose if you consider, up to the end of 1987, as far as I know, there had only been one heart and lung transplant. Jamie Gavin in 1985 became Ireland's first and the world's youngest, and Jamie had a rare disease. In 1988 Robert Wynn a fourteen-year-old from Co. Meath received one. Then on 18th April 1990 Siobhan

Anglim from Wexford had a transplant too so, by the time Gillian received hers in 1990 there had only been two more and both for rare diseases. Looking at these sort of figures, even ten a year might seem a lot.

It was all very worrying, and on top of all the problems we were already coping with, the financial aspect added fuel to the fire. I worried day and night about money from the time Gillian was accepted on the assessment list.

We thought about it constantly but did nothing. I phoned Damian Roberts again and asked him to get some pricing for me. He said that he thought around £3,000 for an assessment to include travel, accommodation and subsistence, but said he would get accurate figures and let me know. Between phoning Papworth Hospital and the Cystic Fibrosis Organisation in London, my phone bills were soaring but what could I do?

As Christmas 1987 approached, I felt it was time to try and sort out finances for the forthcoming assessment. We were now tenth on the list and it was mid-December. Based on two assessments per week we should be off mid-January. I was getting very excited at the thought that Gillian might get a chance to get a transplant. I knew, as Dr Denham said, assessment was step one but still a long way away from a transplant.

I decided to write to the Cystic Fibrosis Association in Dublin, as they were the support group and funded by public money. Although the organisation had been unable to give me any information about transplants the previous summer, they raised money all the time and I felt confident they would be willing to offer some sort of financial support for Gillian.

I wrote to Mrs Maguire, who was the National Co-ordinator of the Association. I explained to her that we were hoping to take Gillian to Papworth Hospital early in the new year, for assessment for heart and lung transplant as she had end-stage lung disease from cystic fibrosis. I told her I thought the whole thing would cost around £3,000 and said we didn't know who was going to pay for it, but was there any facility within the organisation to help with either the medical bills or the other expenses involved in having to go out of the country. It never crossed my mind that there would be a problem. I thought they would be delighted to help, as if Gillian did eventually get a transplant, it would open up the whole thing for other cystic fibrosis children who might be suitable candidates and hence save young lives. To me this is what it's all about.

I wrote in mid-December and received a reply from Mrs McGuire on 7th January 1988. She said she would put my request to the National Executive when they met on 10th January. The next letter said the National Executive were seeking the advice of the "Medical and Scientific Council" and this meeting would not take place until 22nd January. When we received this letter I was very disappointed with the whole tone of things. A simple request for financial support in a life and death situation had received a very bogged down technical reply. They sent children to Lourdes every year, which was lovely, so I couldn't see why they couldn't at least help our Gillian get to London to try and save her life. Brendan shrugged his shoulders and said, "Veronica, that organisation is not interested in you or your child. Why don't you forget about them and stop wasting your time?" He reminded me that when I first mentioned transplant, pounds, shillings and pence flashed across his mind.

It's not in my nature to drop anything mid-stream once I've embarked on it. So I wouldn't just abandon the idea.

I had since been on the phone to London and found out the whole thing would only cost around £2,000 and not £3,000. I wrote to Mrs Maguire on 16th January in plenty of time for the Medical and Scientific Council's meeting on 22nd January to explain the correct costing, so that there would be no misunderstanding. Dr Brian Denham phoned our house on the morning of 11th February. He told Brendan my costing of the assessment to the Cystic Fibrosis Association had been much too high. Brendan told him I had corrected this with Mrs Maguire before the meeting. Dr Denham told Brendan that the Medical and Scientific Council had said heart and lung transplantation certainly was the up and coming treatment for certain selected patients with end-stage cystic fibrosis if they met with the very strict criteria. As an accepted treatment, the actual medical treatment could be funded under the E.112 scheme. This is an E.C. scheme whereby Governments pay for medical treatment not available in one's own country. Dr Denham said the E.112 would not cover travel, accommodation or the many other expenses involved, just the hospital medical bills.

When I came home from school the same afternoon, 11th February, Mrs Maguire phoned me. I didn't know at that stage what Dr Denham had said to Brendan. She spoke about the E.112 and asked if I could come in to see her the following week. I said, "Of course". She asked me to phone her on the Monday. When I phoned her the following Monday I got the impression there had been another change of heart. She didn't mention coming in to see her. She told me to apply to the Eastern Health Board for the E.112 to pay the medical bills and said the other expenses weren't that much. She obviously thought that was the end of Mrs Staunton bothering them.

I was shocked and very disappointed by the whole thing. I just couldn't believe that we, the family of a very sick cystic fibrosis child, were being treated like this by the very organisation that was set up to support cystic fibrosis children.

I sent the following letter to the National Executive.

*Dear Member of the National Executive,*

*I fail to see why it is taking you so long to give me a decision as to whether or not the Cystic Fibrosis Association is prepared to give any funding towards our little daughter Gillian's forthcoming assessment for heart and lung transplantation.*
*I made the request to you before last Christmas, December 1987 and I do think you owe me the courtesy of a written decision on my request.*
*It was from a Doctor I even got the initial information on what was said at the Medical Council meeting regarding Heart and Lung Transplantation. I spoke to Mrs Maguire on the phone twice, 11th and 15th February, and she said the Medical Council's report had not gone back to the National Executive.*
*However, I have heard several things through the grapevine which are quite untrue, one being that "Mrs Staunton is very annoyed because she was turned down by the Medical Council". I was not turned down by the Medical Council because I did not ask them for anything! I asked the C.F. Association.*
*The Medical Council certainly recommended Heart and Lung Transplantation as the up and coming treatment for selected patients and suggested who should pay for the medical end of the procedure. However, we have been told that E.112 will not pay for everything and this is where the Association can help if it so wishes.*
*We have been told by Papworth Hospital that they require the whole family to go over for a four or five day assessment. I can understand Mrs Maguire thinking this is unnecessary as I understand the last C.F. child with whom the Association were involved re. this assessment went to Harefield and only the mother and child went.*
*We have to take our little one to London but hopefully in the next few years it will be possible for Irish C.F. children to have their transplants here in*

*Ireland and hence eliminate the extra expense we are going to have.*
*Remember, the C.F. Association was set up twenty-five years ago to help the children and their families. You are funded by public money and I feel you have a duty to contribute to Gillian's assessment.*
*Many people are asking us if we are getting any funding from the C.F. Association and to date we have to say we don't know.*
*I would ask you to please give me a written reply to my request immediately.*

*Yours sincerely,*

*Veronica Staunton*

Four months after my first request for help the Cystic Fibrosis Association of Ireland sent me a cheque for £200 and specified its use. One air fare and accommodation for a week in London. I thanked them and kept £80 for Brendan's fare and sent them back the £120 as I had already made other arrangements for accommodation and couldn't have an overlap!
This was my experience as it happened when I asked the Cystic Fibrosis Association of Ireland for financial support when we badly needed it to take Gillian to London.
The only light we could throw on this situation came a while later. A meeting took place in the north side of Dublin. Obviously they were discussing transplantation and more cystics had gone for assessment by this time. Someone is supposed to have said, "Look at the way the Stauntons were treated when they looked for help." A lady in the crowd replied, "Ah, but they are a very well off family."
Tom Walsh replied, "Excuse me, what do you know about those people? Do you know them?" The lady said she didn't but she'd heard they were wealthy. Tom said, "Did you know Brendan Staunton's business was wiped out by Hurricane Charlie after being open for just nine months, and they had no insurance?

Don't talk and pass comments about people you know nothing about."

I don't know who gave the impression we were well off and didn't need help. I suppose it's all a question of perception. By some people's standards we are well off. However, there are not many people who are rearing a family nowadays in a position to go flying back and forth to London for transplants.

The truth was, we were broke and in debt after five years of heating our house day and night for ten months of the year. Gillian Staunton never slept one night of her life without heat on all night in her bedroom. One of the reasons she survived, was five years of giving her the best of food and five years of going back and forth to Harcourt Street Hospital many months every year. We were not a wealthy family and would not have asked the Cystic Fibrosis Association for help if we hadn't needed it. In fact, the Cystic Fibrosis Association and the Eastern Health Board are the only bodies or people we have ever asked anything for in our lives. Then it was only when our child was dying. Thankfully we have worked hard and never needed anything from anyone.

My feeling is that organisations funded by public money are there to be objective and treat all children with the disease in the same way. They are not there to be selective in who they help, or get into personalities.

While all this communicating was going on with the Cystic Fibrosis Association I was also in constant touch with Papworth Hospital. The whole assessment programme had slowed down for various reasons and it now looked as if the assessment would be towards the end of March. Gillian wasn't that well at all and was in and out of Harcourt Street every six to eight weeks for IV drugs. It was a very anxious time for all of us.

During my lengthy communications with the Cystic Fibrosis Association I began my association with the Eastern Health Board.

I had previously had illusions regarding the Cystic Fibrosis Association but having read Margaret McStay's book *Colin* I didn't enter into my communications with the Eastern Health Board with any such illusions. Margaret McStay told me she had been naive when she began dealing with the Eastern Health Board. No-one could call me that, as I now had the benefit of her experience. I phoned the Eastern Health Board on 7th March and said I needed an E.112 form to take my sick child to London to be assessed for a heart and lung transplant and where could I pick it up. They sounded quite surprised by my definite attitude. I was told there were forms to be filled in to apply for the E.112. "Don't worry, I can come in tomorrow," I replied. So off I went the next afternoon armed with recent E.S.B. bills and all sorts of private personal information. I knew I had a constitutional right to the E.112 form for the medical bills. But I knew the money for fares, accommodation and to live in London was funded by the 1970 Health Act – an undue hardship scheme for travel expenses to go outside the state for treatment not available here. This part was means-tested. So, I had to be ready to disclose all our business if I wanted to be considered. This was the difficult part. We had never been in this position before.

I was interviewed by a female employee of the Health Board who was accompanied by another lady. I filled in the application for the E.112 first. Then I was asked if I wished to be considered for non-medical expenses and I said, "Yes I did". She explained about the means-test which I understood.

I explained that while the total income looked reasonable we had heavy overheads, mortgage, loans, and heavy oil bills as Gillian required heat twenty-four hours a day. I showed her our E.S.B. bill for almost £200 for two months, as when the oil heating went off at night an electric dimplex took over. I thought I had explained well and had communicated the situation. However, after an hour and a half of filling in forms she commented, "You know Mrs Staunton we don't normally help the middle income group". I reminded her that Barry Desmond, as Minister of Health had said, no family should be out of pocket for having to go out of the country for treatment not available here.

"Oh," she replied, "Is that so, I don't think that's written anywhere."

I left on that note. The next day I wrote into the same person and asked if I could have the E.112 as soon as possible as the assessment could come up at any time.

This particular period, December 1987 to April 1988, when we finally went for the assessment was one of the most stressful of our lives. I felt very disillusioned. Brendan wasn't because he knew money would rear its ugly head. I spent my time waiting and waiting every day for a reply from the Cystic Fibrosis Association and for the E.112 from the Eastern Health Board. Gillian was quite sick and needed hours of extra physiotherapy every day to keep her lungs clear in between hospital admissions. Ironically, with all the treatment that winter, by the time she arrived at the assessment she had picked up again and didn't seem too bad. This is the problem with cystics, they can go through bad patches and then recover quite well.

I waited patiently for five and a half weeks and no E.112 came. Brendan phoned me in school on Friday 15th April and said Papworth Hospital had phoned. The assessment for Gillian's transplant was Monday week, 25th April. I cried with mixed feelings that day. Joy, that she was getting a chance, fear, that she wouldn't be suitable and sadness, that she was sick at all. I still had no E.112! When I came home from school I phoned the Eastern Health Board about the E.112 and I was left on the end of a phone for twenty minutes. I was very nervous because I knew everything hinged on the E.112. If I got it for the assessment and Gillian was suitable for the transplantation then I knew there would probably be no problem. They could hardly give it for an assessment and not for the transplant, although the okay for the actual transplant would have to come from the Minister of Health, Dr O'Hanlon's office. After twenty minutes waiting on the end of the phone I was told a decision had not yet been made on our case.

I was dumbfounded.

This is the treatment I received at the hands of our caring Health Board back in March 1988 and for what reason? I was trying to save my dying child's life.

I was very angry and said "I'm going to London on Monday week and I want that form before then. My child has a constitutional right to this surgery and I will do whatever is necessary to get it for her. I will leave no stone unturned." Gillian looked at me and said "Mum, I'm causing you a lot of trouble."

The following Friday and last post day before we went to London, I still had no E.112. We were desperate. At 7 o'clock in the morning I went down to the main post office in Bray. I explained about the E.112 to the very nice gentleman. He went through the morning post and there it was in a long brown envelope.

"Good luck now, with the little girl. I hope she makes it," said the chap.

The can of worms, if it was one, was open.

# 8. Papworth

Nervous, is the best word to describe how we felt the morning we left Bray, for the long-awaited assessment for a heart and lung transplant for Gillian, in Papworth Hospital in Cambridge, England.

It was 2nd April, over a year, since I had first thought about it, and here we were on a cool Monday morning in April on our way. Una and Dermot picked us up at 5.30 a.m. for a 7 o'clock flight to Luton. Dermot was travelling to London on business but on a different flight. We were all quite sleepy on the journey to the airport. Gillian certainly was not used to being up so early. We were all hoping it would be a successful trip for us. Una really knew how much our hopes hinged on these few days. There had been so much uncertainty about everything for months. The long delay in getting the assessment and the worry about finance had taken another little piece of us, and of course, we had learned more about life and people. I was very disappointed by the attitude of the Cystic Fibrosis Association and could not understand it.

Kelli looked sad as we kissed her goodbye, she would become accustomed to the good-byes over the next few years. We thought the hospital wanted to assess the whole family. We understood the psychological part of the assessment was very important. Kelli was disappointed when they said no, they only meant Gillian and both parents, if possible. It was difficult to explain to a ten-year-old, that we were not going for a holiday in London, but being stuck in a hospital for a week.

When we arrived in Luton we then had a forty minute taxi ride through the English countryside to Papworth. The hospital was set in spacious grounds with a lovely pond and lots of ducks. When

Gillian saw the little ducks she went wild about them. I think she forgot briefly why she was there. Her little face lit up and she kept saying, "Aren't they gorgeous". She was quite at home in Papworth Hospital from the first minute she arrived.

Gillian's room was overlooking the pond, and she had the sliding doors open most of the time, and had little ducks in around her bed. The staff had been a little worried that Gillian would be bored because it was an adult hospital and Gillian, at seven years, was the youngest patient they had entertained. They need not have worried, because she was completely involved with the ducks.

We understood there were lots of tests and many people to meet in the coming days. It was expected we would meet Mr John Wallwork, the surgeon, on Thursday. He would have discussed the test results and other information with his assessment staff. It would be at this meeting, that we would find out whether or not our Gillian would be accepted as a suitable candidate for the transplant.

It was a very interesting, if exhausting and stressful, few days for Brendan and myself. Gillian, for her part, took it all in her stride and enjoyed the attention everyone seemed to be giving her.

On Monday afternoon, a few hours after arriving Virigina O'Brien, a tall, smart, intelligent, no nonsense sort of person came in to see us. She smiled at Gillian who was sitting crossed legged on the bed and she said, "Hello, Gillian and do you know why you are here?"

Gillian replied, "I'm here to see if I will be able to have a heart and lung transplant."

Virginia replied, "But why would you need a heart and lung transplant?" Gillian responded looking her straight in the eyes. "Well, I have cystic fibrosis and it has destroyed my lungs and in another year or two it will get on to my heart and I will die, so this would be a great chance for me."

Virginia just looked at the pretty little seven year old in amazement. She just put her thumb and first finger together and said, "Spot on Gillian".

Virginia told us the schedule for the next few days. She said we must be available each day, all day, to go here, there and everywhere for the various tests. We were told, if someone wanted to see us to talk we had to be there, as everyone was on a busy schedule. So we settled into the small room about 12' x 12' and waited until we were wanted. We took turns going for coffee.

Later Monday afternoon, Brendan went for a walk up the corridor. He heard an Irish accent and turning a corner came upon a man of about fifty, hobbling along with an object in one hand which looked like a battery charger. They got talking and he told Brendan he was from Galway, and as Brendan himself is from Galway a long chat ensued. He said to Brendan, "I just got a new one two weeks ago and I'm only running on two cylinders", and he pointed to the battery-like object. Brendan replied, "You just got a new what?"

"A new heart, the old ticker went on the blink and they gave me a new one."

His name was Vincent Scallon, a very nice Irishman living in England for many years. He told us the night he got his transplant he had been listening to some old Irish records. As a result, he woke up from the operation singing "Paddy McGinty's Goat".

When we left the hospital at 7.50 p.m. that evening to get a meal and return to our accommodation in the village, we left Gillian sitting on the end of Vincent's bed chatting away to him as if she had known him all her life.

The following day was very hectic as most of the tests were carried out on Gillian. Extensive complicated lung function tests were done to determine if there was less than a year of life left. Apart from being psychologically and emotionally suited for a transplant, part of the criteria was that very little time was left. It was a very new treatment, only to be carried out as a last resort when everything else had failed.

We also met several other patients who had already had transplants. We found this very interesting, it really was another world. A young, sturdy, good-looking fourteen year old boy with thick dark hair appeared in Gillian's room and announced, "Hello Gillian, I'm David and I had my heart and lung transplant a year ago". He pulled up his sweat shirt and said, "Here's my scars, but don't worry yours will be neater than this, they had to go back in a second time."

Gillian just looked in amazement. The scar was very heavy and raised up. David and herself had a chat on their own for a while. Now David gave us confidence, he seemed so well and healthy looking.

Another person we met that day was a young man from Bristol, also a cystic fibrosis victim, aged about twenty-two. His name was Steven Brice. He had been transplanted a month previously but still seemed quite delicate and weak. He told Gillian all about the transplant and she was very interested in Steven because he had the same condition as herself. In fact, he came to stay with us in Bray a year later and phones and writes still. He kept saying to Gillian, "I hope you get good bits now, Gillian". I don't think anyone really thought of Gillian as a seven-year-old. She could hold a conversation with the best of them, and knew exactly what she wanted to know. I think the honesty of everyone in Papworth helped us all. People laughed and joked and spoke quite light-heartedly about a very serious subject. This really helped ease the tension.

For the first time, I think Brendan began to feel it really was possible. He was seeing survivors of this procedure rather than just hearing me telling him. Not just statistics, here they were walking around laughing, joking, living with someone else's organs. That evening, when we went to eat, he said to me for the first time, "I hope now they will accept Gillian onto the programme, it would give her another chance." I was very happy that Brendan was coming around to feeling it was possible. Up to this point, I felt he was largely just going along with things to make me happy without any real conviction. He knew we were going to lose the child and was prepared to try anything, but until that second day in Papworth he was not convinced it could happen. As he said himself, he was a farmer's son from the West of Ireland and honestly, left to himself, he would never have even thought about a transplant. Like many other people with a sick child, he would have accepted what the doctors had said.

As we were leaving the hospital the second evening, we met a young Spanish woman called Claire who worked in the hospital. We stood talking for a few minutes, Claire saying how lovely Gillian was and how she reminded her of her little niece in Spain.

We were about to leave Claire when suddenly a blue BMW car with a siren on top came whizzing by us. "Oh, there go the team to retrieve the heart, there's a transplant later tonight", exclaimed Claire.

We were very tired at the close of each day and of course, we were very worried that Gillian might not be deemed suitable for a transplant. We knew for example, if there was anything wrong with her liver or kidneys she would be excluded. Everything had to be just right.

It was a very difficult and complicated operation and all criteria had to be met before anyone was accepted on to the list. We had already waited, hoped and worried for eight months. We knew that if Gillian was accepted, there could still be a long wait until suitable organs were found, or it could be a very short wait. We heard a story of someone heading home to the North of England

after going on the list and the bleep went off half way home and they turned back and had their transplant that very day.
Gillian seemed quite well that week in Papworth and she was very lively. She had been in Harcourt St. several times in the months prior to the trip and had received plenty of IV treatment, but we knew that within a few weeks of going home she could possibly be quite sick again. They were certainly not seeing her at her worst.
On Wednesday morning we were enjoying the sunshine out by the pond. Gillian was trying to catch the little ducks. At one point she ran down a little steep bank after a duck and as she did this , I noticed we were being observed by several nurses, looking down from the second floor of a different wing to the right of us.
We met another transplant patient that day, Jo Hatton, a lovely dark haired young woman in her thirties who had been one of the first few people to get a transplant. She looked very well two and a half years after her transplant. She was back at Papworth, accompanied by her husband, for an out-patient check-up. We didn't spend long talking to her that day as we had to go off for Gillian to have blood taken from an artery, which was the most painful part of the assessment. We exchanged addresses and telephone numbers with Jo and said we would be in touch. At a later date, Jo told me that when she received her transplant she was number six to be transplanted back in 1985. She knew going into the operation that numbers four and five had died shortly after the operation. Not a nice thought going into an operation. Jo was not a cystic fibrosis sufferer, she had had a heart disease since birth. She told us that the first cystic fibrosis patient to receive a transplant had it the same week as herself, Julie Bennett whom we met in Papworth at a later visit. The very first person to get a new heart and lungs at Papworth also came up to see Gillian. She was a mother of two children from the East End of London, a very lively woman in her thirties called Brenda. Gillian was

delighted to meet all these successfully transplanted people and they all seemed to be enjoying life.

By Wednesday evening all the lung function and other tests on Gillian had been completed. We were getting very anxious about our meeting with Mr John Wallwork, the next afternoon. We had spoken to Virginia O'Brien several times during the week. She seemed to have a very central role to play in the assessments. She, like everyone in Papworth was very nice and friendly, but we felt very much the whole time we were being closely observed and scrutinized. One evening, when we had left the hospital for the night, a nurse sat chatting to Gillian. She asked her whose idea it was to look for a transplant and who really wanted it. Gillian told her at the beginning it was her Mum's idea and her Mum who found out all about it. But now, she herself wanted it, because she wanted to live and her Dad also wanted her to live. This nurse also asked Gillian all about her sister Kelli and how her Mum and Dad got along together. Gillian told her we were a very close family and her Mum and Dad got on very well. She told her, both her parents were very active in looking after her, how her Dad didn't go to his business until 10 o'clock and came back at lunch time to see to her. Then Mum came home at 3 o'clock and did the evening shift.

The last thing scheduled for Wednesday evening was a tour of the Intensive Care Unit. Neil Mellon, the head nurse over the Intensive Care staff came to collect us around 7.30 p.m. We had been in the hospital without a decent meal since 9 a.m. and we were very tired and hungry as we embarked on our tour of Intensive Care. As we entered the room we were greeted by a line of about six people, in six beds, hooked up to all kinds of machinery and tubes with a private nurse sitting by or tending each patient. I just didn't want to look too closely as I felt queasy.

Fortunately we stood at a distance and observed while Neil told us what was happening. I pretended it didn't bother me and I think Brendan and myself shared the same sentiment. We remained outwardly cool and calm but we just couldn't wait to get out of the place. Gillian didn't seem to be bothered.

"Now", said Neil, "this room is called "The Bubble" Gillian, and if you get a transplant this is where you will be for the first five days or so. It's a room within a room and is completely sterile. We can only go into the outer room as there is a gentleman in "The Bubble", who has had a heart transplant last night. His name is Brian Amor and his wife has told him you're going to wave in at him. Brendan and myself instantly remembered the BMW whizzing off to get the heart the previous night. We waved in at Brian and I felt very sorry for his wife, Pauline, who was alone and watching her partner fighting for his life. There were machines and tubes everywhere, and he was still on the life support machine. He looked at Gillian through the glass and managed a weak smile and a little wave. I thought about those people all night and wondered why did some people have to go through so much. The next morning his wife Pauline came down to see us and she gave us a card which said.

*May I wish Gillian all the love and luck in the world and you and your husband the courage to get through.*
*Pauline Amor*

She said that Gillian had helped her Brian get through the previous night. He had been feeling sorry for himself until he saw Gillian looking in at him and she said when we left he cried and said, "Here am I feeling sorry for myself tonight, but I had forty-seven years of good life before this. Look at that beautiful little girl of seven, what chance did she ever have?"

When we departed from the Intensive Care Unit, Neil, was going off duty so he said he would drop us off wherever we were going as he had a car. Neil was from Northern Ireland and his wife and four children were still living up in Yorkshire until he made arrangements to bring them down South. He was finding it difficult as property near London was so expensive. He took us to a pub about five miles from the hospital where he said there was great food. Brendan invited him to join us for a drink and some food and he accepted. I think Neil loved his work at the hospital but missed his family. He spoke a lot that evening of the importance of a good nursing team for the direct post-operative care after a transplant. He hinted to us that he didn't think we were quite there yet regarding Gillian and a transplant. He told us you really had to be on your last legs before being accepted on the active list. We spoke a lot about transplants and the type of people who look for them. He said, "Really it tends to be weirdos who go for it." "Thanks", I said and we all laughed knowing he was joking, but meaning – the people generally who go for it are a little different to the average person. We enjoyed the food and conversation and relaxed for a few hours. Neil dropped us back at our accommodation in the village and wished us luck with John Wallwork the following day.

Thursday morning signalled D-Day for us. We would know a lot more by the evening. We arrived at the hospital around 8 a.m. in time to do Gillian's physiotherapy and nebulizer and drugs. After the treatment, Virginia said someone would take us down to see the gym and other parts of the hospital we had not seen already. The reason we were having such a detailed conducted tour of the hospital was to be familiar with it if we came back for a transplant. As soon as we entered the Out-Patient department, we met Joanne Chitteck and her parents. Joanne was eleven and had been transplanted five weeks previously and was now in the halfway house, a flat in the village. We had seen her on the Esther Rantzen T.V. show a few months before, when she was waiting for the transplant. She was Papworth's youngest patient. The family seemed delighted with themselves, especially the fact that they wouldn't have to do the physiotherapy any more. Like Gillian, Joanne was a cystic fibrosis sufferer. We were happy for them and hoped we would be in the same position with Gillian one day soon.

It was not to be! We waited for an hour that afternoon to see Mr Wallwork. Finally at 5 o'clock we entered his office. Mr John Wallwork is a small man with a huge personality. He has a terrific presence, his light blonde hair and piercing blue eyes catch and hold your attention. He was sitting behind his desk when we came in, with a big friendly smile on his face and reminded me of a teddy bear. Gillian sat next to Mr Wallwork looking eagerly at him to see what he was going to say. Brendan and myself and Virginia sat opposite. Virginia had already told us that a decision would have been made based on the assessment, and that decision was final and would not be changed by anything we would say. They were the experts. Mr. Wallwork looked very kindly at Gillian, he was not used to patients a little older than babies. It was easy to see he was a lovely person.

"Yes, Gillian," he said, "you do need a transplant, but not quite yet. We are only doing them on cystics for two and a half years and we have no idea how long you would get out of a transplant. At present you could possibly get longer out of your own lungs than the new ones we could give you. So, we don't want to do it until there is absolutely nothing to lose and you have very little time left. We feel you will be alright for another while. So we are going to put you on our provisional list and when you deteriorate further we will put you on the active list and give you a transplant."

Gillian and Brendan were happy enough with this. Gillian because they were telling her she was alright for another while and could still have it later. Brendan felt okay about it because it gave us breathing space and he was only beginning to believe it could happen and work. He was glad to have time to think about the whole thing. I wasn't happy because I knew they were seeing Gillian during a very good spell after a lot of IV treatment. I knew it could take a long time to find a suitable donor and I would prefer it too early rather than too late. Once something is imminent I would rather get on with it. Now, if they had said, "Come back in five years", I would have been happy. Instead they were saying they would see her again in six months to review the situation. Just more anxious months ahead. Brendan did say, "But Mr Wallwork, what you are saying is, when they are too well they can't have a transplant and when they get too bad, it might be too late. You might not be able to find a donor in time."

"That's right", replied John Wallwork, "Unfortunately we don't always get it right and we do lose people on the list."

He said they were concerned about Gillian's weight which was still hovering under three stone or 18 kilos.

"Try getting her to eat lots of cream doughnuts."

Brendan got edgy at this because only we knew how hard we had tried to get weight on Gillian and how much tube feeding she had received.

"It would take more than cream buns, I'm afraid," replied Brendan.

I kept fairly quiet because I didn't want to show my feelings and I knew we would just have to trust their judgement. I knew everyone was doing their best, but at the end of the day it was our child and we would be the only losers.

It had been a long, difficult, stressful year in many ways since I had first brought up the subject of a transplant. I had a feeling it was going to get worse before it got better. However, at least we were offered some hope, that at some stage, Gillian might get new lungs to prolong her life, if we were lucky and had the stamina to stay the course.

We shook hands with John Wallwork and he gave Gillian a big hug. His parting words were, "The phone is always there and you can use it if you need us." That was very fair.

Gillian said goodbye to the staff and the patients who had been so kind to her all week, but her big regret at leaving was saying goodbye to the ducks! We didn't know if or when we would return to Papworth Hospital. It had been a very interesting, if very exhausting, week in our lives.

*Brendan, Kelli and Gillian in Brennanstown Stables (1986)*

*Gillian and myself in Lourdes (1987)*

# 9. In Limbo

From the day we returned home from the assessment, I felt in an awful limbo. We knew a lot more about transplantation.

"It's like a lotto", remarked Brendan, "So many factors have to gel together to even get to the operating table, and then even after that there is a long road ahead and no guarantees. It could end up being a lot of false hope. On the other hand any hope is better than none."

A month after the assessment, Brendan's father died. He was almost ninety and had enjoyed good health up to two years previously. Loss is loss and age doesn't come into it. We were very sad the day they lowered Pat's coffin into the ground and threw clay in on top of it. He had been a great old man and his greatest qualities had been his kindness and sense of humour. I never heard Pat utter a nasty word against anyone and he used to love Brendan going down to take him out to the pub. He had enjoyed a long, easy–going retirement being spoilt by his large family, spread far and wide through England and America. His greatest tragedy had been the loss of his wife, Brigid, back in 1955. It was the end of an era and Brendan grieved quietly. We left Galway a few hours after the funeral and headed back to Dublin. I thought it would be a while before we would see Galway again!

The effect of the happenings of the past year had left me very very worn out and a little disillusioned. I was very edgy and felt nervous, and everything became such an effort. Little things took on immense significance. Something wrong with the washing machine would throw off my schedule and annoy me greatly. I saw everything as a hassle. Una kept telling me I was tired and drained by the recent events and would feel better when we got the holidays.

Our entry into the world of transplantation had its effect on Brendan, as did Pat's death. When I finished school, Brendan said to me one evening. "Ron, will I close the shop for a week and we'll all go off to Galway for a holiday? We need a break."

I was surprised because we had not been away on holiday since Gillian had been diagnosed. Whenever I would say "where are we going on holiday?" he would reply "Bray Head re-visited".

The only place we had ever gone during all the years was the odd overnight trip to Galway to see Pat. We sometimes took the children in the early years. More recently, my cousin Bernie had kindly offered a few times to have the children as she could do the physiotherapy. It was surprising Brendan suddenly wanted to go to Galway for a full week, and his Dad was no longer there.

We set off on Saturday evening around 7 p.m. and arrived in Galway very late. Michael, Brendan's farmer brother, made a big pot of tea and lots of ham sandwiches when we arrived. Pat's chair sat empty by the range and his hearty laugh was sadly missed. We brought one of his walking sticks home with us as a keepsake when we left. It was a nice relaxing week, apart from the fact that Gillian wasn't that well most of the time. She had no energy and when we went out she just wanted to sleep in the back of the car all the time. Also Brendan nearly died! We had been visiting his Uncle Johnnie in Corrandulla, the other end of the parish and afterwards decided to go to a hotel in a nearby town for drinks and sandwiches. Sandwiches, cokes and a beer were ordered. While we were waiting we heard a glass bang and break behind the bar. Brendan knew the owner of this hotel well but he wasn't there this particular evening. Anyway, the food and drinks arrived. We were all thirsty as it was a hot evening, so we all started to drink first. The children and myself were eating the sandwiches, when quite out of character, Brendan took a sandwich. He wouldn't normally eat sandwiches while drinking a beer. I don't know why he did on this occasion.

While he still had some food in his mouth he took the remaining beer. Suddenly he went purple in the face and choked, gaggled and spat out bread and a large piece of glass, at least two inches long. One more swallow and he would have had a fatal accident. The piece of bread saved him. He said, just as he was about to swallow he felt something in the bread and reacted quickly. We were all shaken. It was truly a frightening experience. Obviously when the glass broke a piece went into one of the clean glasses on the shelf as they weren't turned over. The barman obviously didn't notice as he filled Brendan's pint. The barman was told what happened and the piece of glass presented to him. He played it all down but brought another plate of sandwiches and drinks on the house. Gillian said laughing, "These are much better sandwiches than the first lot, I wonder why?"

From that day to this, Brendan looks very carefully at anything he is drinking. I shuddered when I thought about what could have happened.

We took the children out every day to the beach at Salthill. Gillian and Kelli would play around in the sand for a while but then Gillian would just lie quietly under the umbrella and rest. She never complained but when I asked her was she alright, she smiled and replied, "I'm fine Mum, but I'm very very tired." She would lie and watch all the children running in and out of the water. You notice things more when you are on holiday because you have time to observe what's happening and I suppose people associate being on holidays with children being very active and doing things. We still had to fit in the nebulized antibiotics and physiotherapy and pill taking three times every day.

One day we drove to Knock shrine in Co. Mayo, said a few prayers, visited a friend in Ballyhaunis, had a meal and returned to Galway that evening. It was a pleasant day. Every evening after tea, Brendan and myself went for long walks around the parish of

Annaghdown. We would walk up to the pier and sit on the rocks and talk. Brendan would tell me stories of swimming off the pier as a child. Sometimes we would walk through Michael's fields at the back of the house. It was as if Brendan was taking himself on a journey into his past. One would almost think he knew he would not return for a long time. As we walked through the green fields one evening, he turned to me and said, "Ron, Gillian is going to need that transplant sooner than they seem to think in England. When she goes back in November they will put her on the active list. I'm ready for it now, come what may. We have absolutely nothing to lose but watching her go through the terrible final stage of cyctic fibrosis and in the last weeks of her life gasping for every breath she takes. It's the most awful disease to be inflicted on any family."

I replied, "Yes, I know what you mean, I've felt like that for a long time. I'm glad you really want her to have it. Let's hope she gets the chance."

The week in Papworth had changed his thinking and feelings completely. He knew it was still a very new procedure and a drastic step to take with a young child. However, he had seen people walking around with a good quality of life a few years after a transplant, so why not Gillian? I was so glad Brendan finally felt the same as myself about the transplant and about Gillian's health. It wasn't just me fussing and thinking she was worse than she really was.

Brendan stayed up late at night chatting to Michael, who was really missing Pat very much. They talked a lot about the past. The week seemed to have been good for him apart from the "broken glass" incident. We left Annaghdown on the Sunday morning and have never had a chance to return.

Picking up the post off the mat in our hallway, I began opening one of the letters and realised it was from Dr Denham!

*Dear Mrs Staunton,*

*I have had a very nice letter from Mr Wallwork of the Papworth Unit.*

*They are really very happy with Gillian's respiratory status and there is no doubt on looking back over her data, her lungs have improved greatly in the past two years.*

*Like myself he is concerned about her nutrition and I am pleased that she is at last starting to gain some weight. I would be even more pleased if we could speed this up, I would encourage her to eat hamburgers, cheesecake and everything else to the limit of what she would tolerate, we will give her a further course of nasalduodenal feeding when she next comes into hospital. Her lungs are so good at present that I would be hopeful that we could defer that admission for a good few months.*

*If necessary we will commence her on one of the body building steroids for a while, we can go over the pros and cons of this treatment when you next attend.*

*Mr Wallwork is quite definite that Gillian should not go on the definite list for heart/lung transplant this time, he has placed her on the provisional list and states "because of her age and their recent involvement with Great Ormond Street I think if she needs transplantation in the next two or three years we will probably re-assess her there."*

*They are really just working out the criteria for pre-transplant assessment, I suspect that I will be able to provide him with all the data which he requires in the next year or so and we should do our best to keep the goodwill with both Mr Wallwork's team and the Department of Health so that the door remains open for future use if necessary.*

*Very best wishes.*
*Yours sincerely,*

*Brian Denham FRCPI., DCH.,*
*Consultant Paediatrician*

"So they are not sending her back to Papworth in November as arranged?" I said to Brendan. "No, obviously not", he replied.
He looked very thoughtful as he re-read Dr Denham's letter.
"Well", he continued, "It doesn't matter if she doesn't deteriorate too much, and if there is a drastic change she will go back before November! We'll watch things carefully."
I was very worried that the hospital in England and Dr Denham didn't understand how ill Gillian really was.
I wrote the following letter to Dr Denham.

*Dear Dr Denham,*

*Thank you for your letter of 22nd June regarding Gillian's recent assessment in Papworth for Heart and Lung Transplantation. We are happy that Mr. Wallwork is satisfied with her respiratory status for now.*

*Dr Denham, Brendan and myself are concerned over a few points of Gillian's overall condition. You would probably not be fully aware of the extent to which these things exist but you will know if there is any significance in them and perhaps be able to put our minds at ease.*

*The points in question are.*
*1. The large quantity of coloured mucus which we remove from her lungs three times daily which never decreases and is never clear.*
*2. She runs a temperature of around 100 degrees a huge percentage of the time now.*
*3. Her exercise tolerance is very limited by which I mean any sort of physical activity will leave her tired and inactive for many hours.*
*4. Gillian does not have the stamina to attend school at all. We have tried many times to send her for half days and a few days a week but it doesn't work. Teachers have commented that after a very short time she is tired and just wants to lie down.*

*5. Last but not least, Dr Denham, she has absolutely no appetite 90% of the time and even after her treatment in hospital there seems to be little if any increase in the appetite. We have worked extremely hard on her nutrition over the years but to no avail – we have tried everything to get her to eat and even when we manage to get her to eat quite a lot she doesn't increase in weight. The usual pattern is she hovers around 3 stone all the time and then after x number of weeks she starts to lose weight - you take her in and with the tube feeding she puts back on the weight she has lost and hovers around 3 stone once again. Are we worrying unduly?*

*Best wishes.*

*Yours sincerely,*

*Veronica Staunton.*

The same week we had received Dr Denham's letter, we also received one from the Eastern Health Board. They said the Minister for Health had given them the go ahead to issue an E.112 form for the actual transplant. This was great news but it looked as if we wouldn't be needing it for several years!

Soon after we came back from Galway I went to see Irene Walsh, the girl I had met in Lourdes in 1983, for the day. We had met a few times at the cystic parties at Christmas and spoken briefly about the progress of the children. She thought it was a drastic step to go for a heart and lung transplant. Irene hadn't seen Gillian in about two years and when she saw her that day, in July 1988, she couldn't believe how much she had deteriorated in the two years. I arrived at her door having carried Gill from the station. She thought Gillian looked wretched and I thought her Sean looked super. I would not have known he was cystic at all. It was hard to believe these two children had looked equally well and healthy back in 1983 when we met in Lourdes. Gillian had been battling with Pseudomonas for that six years and Sean hadn't! He had little or no problems with his chest during that time.

I told Irene about the assessment, the fact that they said she would need a transplant but not yet and we didn't know exactly how long before it would happen, if ever. I realised that day, although we were both mothers of cystic children, our lives to date had been quite different. Although they had to do the physiotherapy every day as we did, other than that their life had been more normal than ours. There had been none of the hospitalisation and IV drugs for years, or tube feeding. Sean was attending school full time and playing football and eating well. We had been meeting the cystics in Harcourt Street who, like Gillian, had major chest problems early in life, and by and large were severely affected, so we tended to think all cystics lived the life we had endured over the past six years. It wasn't so, there were many cystics who remained well into their late teens with little disruption to school or family life for many years.

Here was the mother of a cystic child, herself not fully understanding what we were coping with, so how could people with healthy children understand the whole thing? Irene told me afterwards she was amazed that day by the amount of bits and pieces of food I casually withdrew from a bag, pieces of chicken, yogurts, cheese crackers, cans of coke. She said I had all sorts of food and Gillian ate nothing but picked at everything. She thought I had terrific patience and although she knew Gillian looked awful, she hadn't experienced a child just not able to eat and needing lots of encouragement and variety to eat a minimum amount. She also said she thought we must have plenty of money to be able to waste food like this. It was all part of the input into keeping the child going. Today Irene says she understands, because now Sean has Pseudomonas and his appetite is not as good as previously. He is still very well and the Pseudomonas is being treated very aggressively and is not causing too many problems, but she says she can understand more now the way Gillian was carrying on that day in 1988.

We really felt we were continuing to live in a terrible limbo. Gillian needed a transplant but they were not prepared to put her on an active list until she met the criteria of less than a year of life left. We knew she was on the down stretch and a bad pneumonia could kill her instantly. If that happened we would never see London again. We had no choice but to hope and pray everything would work out.

Gillian herself seemed happy enough to be on the provisional list. If the doctors thought she was well enough to wait for a while she was satisfied.

"I don't want it until I really need it, just in case I'm one of the 1 in 10 to die on the table. I don't want to lose any of my time here until there is nothing left and anyway they are getting better at it every year."

She was a rock of sense. She had asked me months previously if everyone woke up after a transplant. I told her truthfully that 10% didn't. I remember she was lying in bed looking at me and she said how many out of ten don't wake up and when I said, "One" she smiled, kissed me and said, "That's quite good, I'll take my chance." She was amazing for her seven years.

The one other incident of that summer of '88 which stood out in my mind was Kelli's ear infection. The two children went swimming in a local indoor pool. Gillian would enjoy the swimming but would come home after the hour and lie on the couch for the rest of the day and then after dinner in the evening go out to play for another while. She had it figured out well. She used what energy she had, to do exactly what she was motivated to do.

Anyway, the girls came home from swimming and later that evening Kelli began to cry with a bad pain in her left ear. She was in severe pain that night and Calpol seemed to have little effect. She was awake most of the night. I sat on the bed and looked at Gillian coughing in one bed and Kelli crying in the other. I said to myself, "God help us."

An ear infection was diagnosed the next day and an antibiotic prescribed. It didn't work and the pain killers were not very effective. We had four more visits by a doctor and several different antibiotics, and ear drops, and all sorts of pain killers, and a week went by and Kelli wasn't getting better. We lost an awful lot of sleep that week. Dr Doyle knew we were all exhausted and had gone through a tough year. She had given me a letter for a specialist a few weeks earlier for Kelli, as she had been having heavy nose bleeds. She suggested we would ask for an emergency appointment and have the ear looked at as well. The consultant in the Blackrock Clinic said he would have to take Kelli in as a day patient, put her to sleep, cauterise her nose and clean out the deeply embedded ear infection. "Otherwise you will have prolonged problems." It was a very successful procedure and it was great to see Kelli out of pain. It cost the best part of £500. We were not in the Voluntary Health Insurance and not for the first time we topped up a U.D.T. loan.

This year of 1988, to date, had been our most taxing and stressful in coping with Gillian's long difficult illness.

I went back to school in September for two days, and found I was gasping for breath as I tried to teach. Under my doctor's orders, I took six weeks off work and slept day and night during that time. I was absolutely exhausted.

The doctor said if I didn't slow down and pace myself I would become seriously ill. The fact that I was able to sleep so much frightened me and made me take a close look at the pace I had been living at. Taking the initiative completely, having to negotiate the whole transplant assessment, the worry over finance and lack of support, in between teaching and looking after a seriously ill child had taken its toll on my health.

By the end of 1988 Gillian would have been hospitalised six times in the year! I would like to have stopped teaching at this point but this was financially out of the question. We needed both of us working to survive the financial input required to keep Gillian alive until we could hopefully get her a transplant. We were already servicing a big mortgage and several loans accumulated over the years of sickness and long spells in hospital. I went back to school well rested and ready for whatever was ahead.

In September Dr Denham had put Gillian on a two month course of anabolic steroids. This stimulated her appetite, be it artificially, and she ate all before her, thousands of extra calories every day. It was a pleasure to see her eat. It stretched her tummy and made meal times much more pleasant for the family. She put on about 10lbs in weight and looked well. We began to relax and feel maybe she would be alright for a few years. What in fact was happening was the outward appearance improved while her lungs rotted away inside. We were fooled by her appearance.

# 10. More Assessments – Active List

It now seemed unlikely Gillian would need a transplant in the immediate future. We decided we should renovate Brendan's shop and make it unisex to stimulate more business. We felt we had been coasting too long. Directly after Christmas, we went to see our bank manager to arrange funds to renovate and stock the new ladies' section.

In the first week of January 1989, we combined a routine visit to Harcourt Street for lung function tests with a visit to the Hair Suppliers to buy hood dryers and stock for our new venture. There was some delay with the lung functions so Dr Vivien Murphy said, "Go ahead Veronica and take care of your business, we'll look after Gillian until you and Brendan come back."

Off we went and two hours later returned to pick up Gillian, the car laden down with gear for the new shop. Brendan waited outside on the steps of the hospital thinking I would return immediately with Gillian. However, we were in for yet another surprise. Vivien said she'd like to see me for a minute. "Veronica, Gillian's lung function has dropped dramatically. I think we'll have to get her back to Papworth as soon as possible." I couldn't believe it and immediately thought of all the hair equipment in the car. Gillian ran off ahead of me to tell Brendan she had to return to Papworth. Vivien said she would speak to Dr Denham and Papworth Hospital, and be in touch. Vivien had always been very supportive and worked very hard with all the cystics.

We decided that night we would go ahead with our plans for the shop in spite of this new development. I would take Gillian back to England on my own. We had obviously been fooled by how well

Gillian was looking from the weight she had put on as a result of the anabolic steroids. The physical appearance shielded the rapid deterioration of the lungs inside her.

Two weeks later, while arrangements were being made with London, Gillian became ill and was admitted to Harcourt Street once again for IV treatment for her lung infection. She spent three weeks in hospital, we went back and forth every evening. When she came out of hospital we had a date for our return to England, 28th February. However, she didn't make it back to England without more IV treatment. A week later with only a week to our departure for England, I had her back in Dr Denham's clinic. He asked me to do a week of IV at home myself and then continue for the week in England. Home IV was becoming popular so that the children could be at home more. I hadn't done it because I was working and didn't feel up to it on top of all the physiotherapy.

The week before our departure was one of the most hectic and stressful of our lives. The ladies section of the Dargle Hair Studio had opened so Brendan was very busy. Gillian was very ill and needing physiotherapy four to five times a day. Every few hours she would be choking from the build up of phlegm and the physiotherapy was the only way of giving her relief and easing her breathing. She was receiving the IV drugs three times a day. She just lay on the couch lifeless in between treatments. We were very worried and I was not looking forward to taking her to England on my own. I began to wonder was it all a waste of time. However, I had seen Gillian ill many, many times and she always bounced back.

Gillian and myself left Dublin Airport on Monday 27th February 1989 not knowing how long we would be away. We were also going to Great Ormond Street Children's Hospital after the Papworth assessment. They had more experience with young children and had just started doing the heart and lung transplants the previous July.

There was no running around after ducks on this occasion. I pushed Gillian everywhere in a buggy or carried her, she was breathless after walking about ten yards. I kept thinking if only she had gone on the list the previous year. The staff at Papworth knew immediately Gillian had deteriorated a lot within the ten months since they had seen her. However, she still had her lovely smile and sense of humour. Nothing ever took that away from her. She was worried about me having to walk back through the lonely village to where I was staying. She need not have worried because on Monday afternoon Virginia O'Brien, who had been so impressed with Gillian on our first trip, gave me the address of my accommodation and said, "Gwen Mullan, a lady from Northern Ireland whose daughter is waiting for a transplant is also staying in the same house as yourself."

Gwen and myself became friends immediately. She was lovely and her twenty -year-old daughter Carolyn, a cystic fibrosis sufferer like Gillian was beautiful. Carolyn had been on the active list for three months and was back for a review. We were great company for one another that week, and it was nice to hear about another family in a similar situation to ourselves. Gwen kept telling me Gillian would go on the active list no problem, she kept saying, "The poor wee thing, isn't she lovely." Our stories were quite different. Carolyn had been diagnosed as an infant.

"Veronica, the doctor handed the wee baby to me and said, 'Be good to her, she won't live long.'" This is what Gwen told me over coffee the first night we met. I felt as if I had known Gwen all my life within a few hours. She went on to tell me that she didn't have the heart to ever tell Caroline she had cystic fibrosis. I was fascinated. "What do you mean you didn't tell her, didn't you do physiotherapy and wasn't she sick a lot?"

"No, Veronica, she wasn't sick much. She went to school and grew up and not a word about anything. She found out by accident when she was eighteen," went on Gwen. I couldn't believe what I was hearing.

"She was in the out-patients department of our local hospital for some trivial reason and the nurse said, "Oh, you're the wee girl who has cystic fibrosis." Gwen said Carolyn ran off to her friend and said, "Jenny, I've got cystic fibrosis." The friend replied. "Carolyn, if you had cystic fibrosis you would be dead."

Gwen said that Carolyn was furious with Harry and herself for never telling her. It was an awful shock which she found very difficult to cope with. Soon afterwards, Carolyn began getting a lot of chest infections, and her condition deteriorated rapidly within two years. Gwen told me that Carolyn was watching Terry Wogan one evening and he was interviewing John Wallwork and a lovely young girl, Lisa, who had cystic fibrosis and had a heart and lung transplant. She came running out to me and said, "That's exactly what I need, a heart and lung transplant. You can go off and get me one."

Hence, Gwen and Carolyn were here in Papworth on the active list waiting for a transplant.

When I told Gwen about Gillian's background and the number of hospital admissions over her short eight years she was very upset. "Ach, it's not fair Veronica, how did you manage at all?"

At this point I would have thought Gillian was sicker than Carolyn, although Carolyn was already three months on the active list. We had been told they would only put Gillian on the active list when it was deemed there was less than a year of life left. I think the criteria might be slightly different for young children than young adults. They are very reluctant to transplant a young child unless death is imminent.

I was familiar with the hospital and the routine of the assessment, which made it easier, but I really missed not having Brendan with us. He would always throw some humour on any situation.

The days were very busy because in between the lung functions and all the assessment tests, Gillian still had to have her physiotherapy, nebulizer and IV drugs three times every day. Her veins were bad from all the strong IV drugs and every day that week the vein would "tissue" and the needle would have to be re-sited. This meant waiting for a doctor to come up and try to find a good vein to re-site the needle before she could receive her drugs. Gillian's arms were full of bruises from failed attempts to get needles into her veins. She never complained and would pick out veins and show the doctor where the good ones were. After all the years I still hated to see anyone poking around my little one's arms with needles.

Thursday dawned cold and wet. Gwen and Carolyn were leaving for Belfast at lunch time. Gillian and myself were due to see Mr Wallwork when he was free but we were not leaving for Great Ormond Street until the following morning. Gwen was hoping we would have seen Mr Wallwork before they left. She was very anxious to know if Gillian was transferred onto the active list. I told her I would phone her later if we missed them. At 10 a.m. we were summoned up to wait for Mr John Wallwork. We waited in a small room with three other people ahead of us, all waiting to see the surgeon. No-one spoke and the tension in the room was unbelievable.

Everyone just sat there silently and solemnly, as if they were all awaiting a death sentence. The deadly silence prevailed for about half an hour. At one point I left the room and walked Gillian slowly up the corridor, just to get away from the terrible tension. When we came back a young girl of about fourteen was saying to her mother and father, "But I'm telling you I don't want any transplant, you can't force it on me."

Finally it was our turn to meet Mr Wallwork for the second time within a year. I just didn't know what he was going to say! In contrast to the previous meeting there was very little discussion. His bright, intelligent, warm, friendly face focused on Gillian. He directed his question at the child. "Well young lady, how have you been?"

"Not the best", replied Gillian.

"Yes, I know Gillian, you need new lungs and you need them soon! We are going to try and get you sorted out as soon as possible."

Gillian hugged him hard, her face beaming and she said to John Wallwork, "Thank you." Dr Smith, the cystic fibrosis doctor smiled at Gillian.

Gillian couldn't wait to get out of the room to phone her Dad and tell him the good news. Mr Wallwork explained, we would be on the lists at Papworth and Great Ormond Street and we would have the transplant in either hospital depending on circumstances, when suitable organs became available. He said either himself or Mr de Leval would do the transplant.

I said, "Brendan has his confidence in you." To which he replied, "And I have my confidence in Mr de Leval."

He knew how attached Gillian was to himself and Papworth. He said if it was at all possible it would be done in Papworth by him. I shook his hand warmly and said, "Thank you very much." I felt we were now really on our way and Gillian was going to get a second chance. Gillian gave him another big hug and said, "See you soon, I must phone my Dad."

Gwen and Carolyn were waiting for their taxi when we returned to the ward. Gwen took Gillian's face between her hands and cried. She was just so happy for us, such a warm person. I was delighted we had met Gwen and Carolyn and we have kept in touch ever since. Gwen said she thought Virginia was wary of putting us both in the same accommodation, as we were from Northern Ireland and Southern Ireland. If that was so she needn't have worried.

Because Gillian was now on the active list, blood had to be taken to give them various other information for the computer. Gillian and myself were very excited that day and Gillian said it was the best day of her life. She said, "There is hope. I will get a second chance to live". We told everyone we met Gillian was now on the active list. I didn't want to go near Great Ormond Street at all. We both just wanted to get home and get ready to return for the transplant. Brendan was phoned many times that afternoon and evening.

We left Papworth early the next morning in a hospital car for the fifty mile journey to Central London. We were told there would be some tests done on Friday and we would meet some of the team. We would then have to wait until Monday for the rest of the assessment. Everything would be completed by Monday or Tuesday. I had phoned some old friends who lived just outside Central London and it was arranged that Ray would pick us up on Saturday evening and take us out to their home until Sunday evening.

Gillian was absolutely exhausted after all the tests in Papworth and I didn't know how she would stand up to any more tests, needles or blood taking. As the car approached London I immediately felt overwhelmed by the noise and the sheer speed of the traffic. I thought back to my student days and how I had enjoyed everything about London. How time and life can change one. Little did I know in those carefree days of student life and theatre going, the mission on which I would one day return to the capital. In the midst of the excitement of Gillian going onto the list an awful sadness came over me.

We arrived at the hospital around noon and immediately began meeting various members of the assessment team. Mary Goodwin, the liaison sister was one of the first people we met. The conversation had hardly begun when Gillian said, "I want my transplant at Papworth, I don't like it here". Mary joked with Gillian and tried to explain all the advantages of a children's hospital but Gil was adamant. I had never before seen her so anti and negative about anything, on that first day in Great Ormond Street. Ian Martin, the transplant co-ordinator came to see us next and he got the same reception from Gillian but he persisted and did a few tricks which seemed to impress her and she joked back. When he thought he had won her over she said, "Well, it's okay here and you are all very nice but I still want it at Papworth." I was mortified and didn't know what to say.

I think it was the setting of the hospital she disliked more than anything. She liked looking out at the pond of ducks rather than large dirty grey buildings and lots of noise. We were not used to the centre of London. I didn't like the setting myself but wanted as many options open for Gillian as possible. Dr Scott in Papworth had said to me, "Her best chance is in Great Ormond Street".

They knew she was ill and had already had a difficult week so they only did a very limited assessment. A lot of the test results from Papworth were transferred to Great Ormond Street's transplant programme. It had been in operation for nine months at this time and there was a lot of co-operation between Papworth and themselves. I think John Wallwork had assisted at several of the heart and lung transplants in that first year. The staff seemed much more prepared to discuss the number of transplants, length of waiting time and in general were more forthcoming than Papworth. Being a children's hospital obviously had a bearing on the whole approach.

It was another complete adjustment for us, and an awful effort to concentrate on what people were saying to us that first Friday afternoon in Great Ormond Street. I had heard so much down through the years about the world famous hospital I should have had an interesting experience, but I was in such a daze experiencing very mixed emotions about everything, all I could think of was getting home to Brendan and Kelli.

I slept on a pull out bed next to Gillian on the ward that night. We had the four bedded room to ourselves. On Saturday morning, although not well at all, Gillian insisted on going to see the pigeons in Trafalgar Square. We took a taxi there and then I pushed her around in the push chair. When we ran out of bread for the pigeons, Gillian opened up one of her capsules of Creon which she used to digest her food and held the little minute round balls of enzymes in her hand to attract the pigeons. They came and ate Creon from her hand and she laughed loudly. She looked wretched but was still very determined to enjoy the week-end and make the most of being in London. "In case I don't ever come back", she said.

Next we went to the Planetarium which she really enjoyed, always having a fascination with the stars and night time atmosphere. Then we had a meal and I pushed her all the way back to the hospital in the push chair.

After sleeping for several hours, Gillian rested on her bed and chatted to me about the morning. A doctor whom we had met in Papworth the previous year came up to chat to us, Dr Peter Helmes, the cystic fibrosis specialist. He was a lovely, quietly spoken man with a twinkle in his eye. I think he thought we might find it lonely in the hospital at the week-end with everyone gone. We told him how we had spent the morning, and how that night, friends were taking us out to their home until Sunday evening. Gillian told him she had given the pigeons Creon and they both laughed. Dr Helmes kept us company for a while and told us about his own family and asked about Kelli. He really made us feel at home. By Saturday evening Gillian seemed to be getting used to Great Ormond Street.

Ray and his eldest daughter, Niamh, picked us up that evening and brought us out to their home in Brockley, about fifteen minutes from Central London. Ray promised Gillian that on the way back on Sunday evening he would give her a late night conducted tour of all the sights.

We all sat around the table for a meal that night, my first meal in a house in a week. I looked around at Ray and Maggie's four lovely healthy children. Turlough, a tall handsome boy of fifteen. Niamh, thirteen with lovely long dark hair, a picture of health, Cora, eleven with light skin, blue eyes, long blonde hair and last but not least Aoife, nick-named Fifi, aged six, absolutely beautiful, bubbling with energy and life, a very outgoing child. I hadn't seen Maggie and Ray since Brendan and myself spent a week-end in London with them back in 1977 but Gillian and myself immediately felt at home and were delighted to get out of the hospital atmosphere.

Maggie is a nurse and she kept looking at Gillian with the cannula in her arm. I'd say she realised how lucky Ray and herself were to have four lovely healthy children. The older children were very aware of Gillian's condition but Fifi wanted Gillian to play with her and couldn't understand Gillian's quietness. The contrast between the four Stone children and Gillian was a stark reminder of the situation. I was asking Turlough and the girls what they wanted to be when they grew up and they were telling me their hopes for the future. Gillian said she wanted to be a singer or a model. There was no question now in Gillian's mind that she might not get the call or a transplant might not work. It was positive thinking all the way for Gillian.

I think Maggie felt if we didn't get the call pretty soon we wouldn't need it. She didn't think Gillian was at all well. It was difficult to digest that she had less than a year to live. We spoke that week-end as if we would be back for the transplant within weeks or a few months.

To date, seven heart and lung transplants had been carried out in Great Ormond Street since the previous July. We were told the average wait had been around three months. Zoe Jackson, a beautiful fourteen year old girl had been the first and her Mum told me they only waited ten days. In fact, after two days on the list they had a donor but it transpired the organs were unsuitable. So she had her assessment and transplant within two weeks. I had asked about all the children who had been transplanted and how they were doing. I loved to hear about other children's success and now hoped we would join that list soon.

The experience of having Gillian in their home affected Ray and Maggie's children. I spoke to Maggie a week later and she said the night we left, her four children just sat around the table and cried for Gillian. She said they got really upset that such a lovely young girl had already gone through so much and had so much ahead of her. They couldn't get over how accepting and placid Gillian was about the whole thing. The thought of anyone so young having to face something as big as a heart and lung transplant overwhelmed them, to see that life isn't all a bed of roses. They had heard me doing the physiotherapy and saw the amount of treatment Gillian had to endure daily to survive each day.

During the few days in Great Ormond Street we met a boy of fourteen who had his transplant a month before. His name was Michael Herron and he was also cystic. Michael looked very well and was very lively. He waved at Gillian from a distance but wouldn't come too close because she had Pseudomonas. His Dad Eamon came and chatted to Gillian for a long time and told us all about the transplant experience they had just gone through. Another young teenage boy was in intensive care, a few weeks after his transplant, also cystic, but things were not going well for him. We didn't see John but spoke to his Mum and Aunt and they looked very tired and worn out with the whole thing. We also made friends with the play leaders, Karen and Janet, and another lovely chap David, who had a heart condition himself and worked as a volunteer in the hospital.

On Monday we met Mary Goodwin and Ian Martin again, and, having completed the tests, were told we could leave that evening. We were delighted to be going home to Brendan and Kelli and now we had new hope that Gillian's life could be extended and she could possibly even get some better quality of life than she had ever experienced. Wouldn't it be a miracle if it happened?

*Gillian and friends (April 1990)*

# 11. Trial Run

It had been a long, mostly lonely, period of uncertainty and anxiety, since I had first thought about the possibility of a heart and lung transplant for Gillian back in the winter of 1986. Many people had thought I was just dreaming. I think they thought if it helped me survive what was happening to my young child, to dream about a transplant, then there was no harm in my fantasy. I also think some people felt sorry for me, that I didn't seem to be able to accept losing Gillian, just as many people before me had lost their children from cystic fibrosis. When I had first said to people, "I am going to try and get a heart and lung transplant for Gillian in England," they would look at me and smile, nod their heads and say things like, "Are you really, that would be nice."

I soon stopped talking about it outside Una and my own family. Una had been a great source of support for me right from the beginning. She had helped Kelli by taking a big interest in her and starting her off with the music and later picking out the flute as her instrument. Kelli had spent many nights in Una's home over the years. Una had spent time taking me into the hospital visiting Gillian. But more than anything else, she cared, and she listened to me talking things through for endless hours. Before I had mentioned transplant to Brendan, Una had discussed it with me. There were times Brendan coped with cystic fibrosis by not talking about it at all. He didn't want every day to be a cystic fibrosis day or in fact a transplant day. He did his utmost to keep humour and calmness in our lives through it all.

Once Gillian went on the active list for the transplant we all tried to prepare ourselves for the inevitable and drastic changes in our lives. That we were now on the active list was like being at the starting point of a race. To get to this starting point had taken almost two years. We were very excited and full of confidence in March 1989, that we would win the race. It was a race against time to get to the operation. We couldn't even think beyond getting the transplant. What would happen afterwards was another stage to be faced. Waiting for a transplant is completely different to waiting for any other operation. You might have to wait for any operation but there is an end in sight, because if it becomes an emergency it can be done immediately. With a transplant there is no end in sight, no time to pin your hopes on. You are waiting and your life is depending on it but it may happen or it may not. It may be a week, a month or a year and you don't have much time. You have absolutely no say at all. If a suitable donor becomes available in time you get your chance. A child somewhere has to die!

It had been pointed out to us at Papworth that you are not hoping for another person to die to save your child. Tragedies happen, and you are asking someone to give your child the gift of a chance to live, by giving something their own child doesn't need any more. But still, there was a sadness for us knowing there had to be a death of another child for Gillian to get this life-saving surgery.

A few days after we returned from England, Virginia O'Brien from Papworth Hospital phoned. She said we would need a bleep so that we could be alerted if we were not home when the call came. Time would be of the utmost importance. With heart and lungs, unlike other organ transplants, the lungs must be inserted within four hours of extraction from the donor. Virginia told me she couldn't give us a British Telecom bleep as it wouldn't work here. She told me to call the Cystic Fibrosis Association in Dublin and ask them to get me one.

"£150 is a nothing for an organisation and this is very important", commented Virginia. I laughed and said, "Virginia, I don't think the Dublin branch of the Cystic Fibrosis Association will be willing to get me a bleep." She replied, "Why not? Tell them the Transplant Co-ordinator from Papworth Hospital said it's an emergency."

It took a week for me to contact Mrs Maguire in Cystic Fibrosis headquarters. She was out several times when I phoned and did not return my calls. Finally, when I did speak to her and explained what Virginia O'Brien had said, her answer was, "Well she shouldn't have said that, it's nothing to do with us". I answered, "Who is it to do with then?" She then arranged for us to be supplied with a bleep.

The bleep unit number was 4560 and if it activated and you didn't hear the message you phoned the company in Dublin and asked if there was a message for Unit 4560. The message we were anxiously waiting to hear was "Please phone Papworth Hospital" or, "Please phone Great Ormond Street Hospital". I carried the bleep with me everywhere I went. It sat on my desk in school during the day and in my pocket or handbag at all other times.

The first month was great, we were ready with a case of new clothes packed for Gillian. People kept saying things like,"Did you hear anything yet?" or "Do you think you will go soon?"

We really thought it would happen very quickly. Ian had told me they were often offered organs several times a week. It was a matter of the correct blood group. If two people on one list had the same requirements exactly, a conference of the transplant team would be held, to determine the sickest person, and length of time on the waiting list would obviously be a factor.

When Gillian went on the list, there were about forty on Papworth's list, Gillian being the youngest by a number of years, and seven on Great Ormond Street's list. There was no-one else on either list with the same requirements as Gillian.

One Sunday afternoon, we went with my parents to meet an aunt of mine for afternoon tea in a hotel. While we were chatting, Kelli and Gillian noticed a lady sitting down with a lovely little Pekinese dog on her knee. Straight away they started up a conversation and started stroking the little dog.

"We are getting a dog like him after Gillian gets her transplant", Kelli explained to the lady. Within minutes Kelli had told Brenda Ryan all about Gillian. They exchanged phone numbers and Brenda said she would let them know where to get a little Pekinese.

Brenda went home and told her teenage daughter Mary all about Gillian. Within a week our phone rang and Brenda told me her daughter, Mary, and her friends in Killiney had bought a little Pekinese puppy as a present for Gillian. We met them on Easter Monday and Gillian was bursting with excitement. She said that she hoped she didn't get the call until she had a few weeks with "Lucy".

This gesture of kindness from these people was lovely. They will never know how happy they made Gillian at that difficult time. It made us realise that there are people who do care.

We were driving through the town of Bray one Monday evening in April when suddenly the bleep in my bag activated. The message was muffled coming through the bag. I was so surprised I swerved the car. Brendan exclaimed, "Calm down, Ron, or we'll all be donors."

I immediately pulled over the car at a phone booth and phoned the company for the message. It was a mistake! The person who previously had our unit number still had customers who obviously didn't know their number had been changed. Gillian said, "Phew", when I came back to the car and said it was a mistake.

We lived on a high those first few months after going onto the active list. There was hope and something to look forward to for Gillian. She was really delighted with herself. The six weeks of IV treatment had done her good and she was once again able to walk around. She would sit on a little pillar at the top of our road and wait for Brendan to come home at lunch time with all sorts of goodies for her. She would place her order on the phone and Brendan would bring her exactly what she wanted to eat. Since Dr Denham had put her on the course of anabolic steroids six months previously her appetite had been good. It remained good even when the steroids stopped. However, no matter what she ate she didn't put on weight. When she was on the steroids she went from around 3 stone or 18 kilos to 3 stone 10 lbs or 24 kilos, and when she came off the steroids it remained static. A patient cannot be on steroids 6 months prior to a transplant.

On the 3rd May, Brendan and Gillian went off to see the "Ultimate Event" – Frank Sinatra, Sammy Davis and Liza Minnelli. I got the tickets as a surprise for Gill and Brendan who were both great fans of Sinatra. Gillian had been listening to his records for years. Brendan was terrified taking Gillian into such a huge crowd but I said, "Go ahead and let her enjoy herself, most of her life has been spent in hospital." So off they went and it was a fabulous evening for them. Kelli and myself met them in a hotel afterwards. This was an early birthday present for Gillian's forthcoming ninth birthday. Gillian talked about the concert for weeks and said Liza kept it going. It was a night to remember for her. People said Brendan was brave to take a child like Gillian to such a concert but it was lovely to see her enjoying herself.

As the first few months passed, and the phone never rang, and the bleep didn't go off, we began to get a little anxious again. Were we going to remain at the starting point and never move forward? However, Gillian was still stable and we felt we had some time, although we knew how unpredictable cystic fibrosis was.

I would phone Mary Goodwin in Great Ormond Street or Virginia O'Brien in Papworth once in a while and just ask how things were and if they had done many transplants. Mary would tell me how many they had done and how old the children were and how they were doing. I loved to hear children were getting them and felt, soon it would be Gillian's turn.

It happened in the final week of the school year, Monday 26th June, Brendan had dinner ready as he always did on his day off. After dinner and a cup of tea I decided to go for a little nap as I often did those days. At 4 o'clock I said to Kelli, "Don't disturb me for any reason for the next hour Kelli. I'm very tired. I'll phone anyone back if there are any phone calls."

At 4.30 p.m. Kelli shook me and said, "Sorry to waken you Mum but there's a man called Ian from Great Ormond Street Hospital on the phone and he said you will want to speak to him." Mary Goodwin had phoned to see how we were coping a few weeks before so I didn't take much notice but groped my way down to the phone half asleep. I soon woke up when Ian Martin asked how Gillian was and then continued, "What would you say if I told you we have potential organs for her?"

I thought Ian was joking at first but soon realised he was very serious. He told me they wouldn't be 100% sure until later that night but based on the information they had, we were to fly over on the last flight and surgery was scheduled for 10 a.m. the following morning. I must have gone into shock because I remained very calm and just said to myself, "This is it Veronica, come what may it's out of our hands." Things moved quickly after that. Dr Denham phoned and said he had booked the flight for 8.30 p.m. He spoke to Gillian and wished her luck but reminded her that although we were going over, it would not be finalised until later that night. I then phoned Una who was going to drive us to the airport and look after Kelli. I just said to Una, "We got the call, we need to leave for the airport within an hour and a half." She just said, "I don't believe it."

Brendan went down to get my parents. I phoned Kay McDonagh, Gillian's home teacher and a friend and colleague of mine. Kay and Gillian were close and she said she was on her way over.

I started to throw everything I owned into a case saying to myself, "Gosh I might be gone for months. I don't know." Gillian's case was all ready and had been ready for the past three months. I told Kelli to come home when she returned from the airport, and get her things packed, go to school every day and not to worry and keep things as normal as possible for herself. Kelli just kept saying, "Will Gillian be alright, will I ever see her again?" Gillian just laughed and said, "Don't worry Kelli, I'll be fine, this is my chance."

It crossed my mind briefly that this could possibly be the last time my two girls would be together. However, I didn't let that thought linger for too long. At that point, everyone seemed to descend on the house together and the phone never stopped ringing, so there was no more time for any more conversation with the girls.

I helped Brendan pack his case. The plan was that he would stay in London for a week or so, or until Gillian was out of intensive care. He would then return home to Kelli and his business and try to keep things going here. Brendan seemed in a muddle that evening, and usually he was very calm. Una noticed how calm I was and I think she was surprised. She said to someone, "Just wait until it all hits her."

Finally we were more or less ready to head for the airport. My parents said goodbye and good luck and hugged Gillian with tears in their eyes. They took Lucy, Gillian's little dog and the love of her life, home with them to look after until Brendan came back. Kay also hugged Gillian and said goodbye.

The last thing Brendan did before he left the house was to plonk the dreaded bleep on the kitchen table and say "Thank God that's the end of that thing, it's been dreadful."

If only he had known what was going to happen.

As we closed the front door I thought, "God knows when I'll see my home again. The journey to the airport was a little morbid, we were all quiet and subdued. Just the odd comment broke the silence. Brendan chirped, "Well, we will only do this particular journey once in our life. Imagine this time tomorrow it will be all over."

I was unusually calm and showed very little emotion. I was floating, we could have been going shopping in Dublin. I was playing it all down in my mind because it was too big to even acknowledge. In retrospect, we were completely unprepared for a transplant. The final evidence of that came when we arrived at the airport.

I wrote a cheque for three single tickets. We had £150 cash and an overdrawn cheque book and Visa card! Our plight was referred to as a medical emergency and we were taken straight through to the plane. I think some people booked on the flight had to be rescheduled. The staff on the plane knew where we were heading for and observed us sympathetically. Gillian was taken up to the cockpit to see how the plane was navigated and have a look around. She was delighted. The whole thing just seemed so unreal.

In London, a chap from Aer Lingus put Gillian into a wheelchair and took us off to hand us over to the ambulance which had come from Great Ormond Street. As he pushed her around the airport he asked us what the problem was. When he heard Gillian was heading for a heart and lung transplant he said she was a great kid. He wished us luck as we climbed into the ambulance. The journey to the hospital was a silent one because it was now 11.00 p.m., and we were very tired and very much in a daze. Mary Goodwin had left a message to phone her if we needed her, no matter how late and she would come over to see us. I told the nurse we were fine and not to bother Mary. It was after midnight. I thought I wanted to go to sleep! However, there were lots of forms to fill in and permission slips to be signed, and blood to be taken. Gillian received a dose of Cyclosporin, the anti-rejection drug. Brendan and myself were given a room along the corridor from Gillian for the night on a pull-out bed. We were told we would be moved down to the parents quarters in the basement the next day. We met a lovely Irish nurse called Brigid Conway.

As I did Gillian's physiotherapy and nebulizer that night I thought I would never do it again whatever happened. It looked as if the transplant would go ahead at 10.00 a.m. the following morning, 27th June. A doctor told us all the tests but one had been completed on the donor and everything was fine. At 2.30 a.m. Brendan kissed Gillian and went off to bed. I intended following within minutes but stayed with Gillian for about fifteen minutes. We said her night prayers as usual and a special prayer for the family of the little boy who had just died. I thought a lot about the donor family and the fantastic people they must be to even think of anyone else when they had lost their little boy. All donor families are very special people in my opinion. Finally, I kissed Gillian and told her I would wake her at 7 o'clock. Brendan was already snoring when I joined him. Twisting and turning for the next hour, and thinking over everything that had happened that day, sleep would not come to me. Finally, I ached to see Gillian again, so I slipped out of bed, and crept back along the corridor to her room. My little baby was fast asleep and she looked beautiful. Sitting by her bed I stayed for a full hour just looking at my little nine year old, who had lived such a long hard difficult nine years, yet remained cheerful, happy, grateful and oh so loving. Gillian always thought I could always make everything turn out alright for her. She was close to Brendan but absolute oneness would be the best way to describe our relationship. As I looked at

Gillian that night I felt she and we together had fought every day of the nine years to have her for another day. It had been a daily battle for survival for what by other people's standards would be considered bad quality of life. But it was our life together and we cherished it. We had thought it so worth fighting for that we were here this night in a strange hospital, in a strange country surrounded by strangers, and a strange family in their own grief were prepared to give Gillian not only a chance to extend her life but improve its quality.

That particular night as I kept my silent vigil over Gillian in the silence of the night I thought of all cystic fibrosis families everywhere. I thought of the difficulties brought on people by this awful, soul-destroying disease, which had wrecked many families through death, and their failure to stand up to its demands. Not all would ever be as lucky as us to get the chance of a transplant. I hoped and prayed that a cure would soon be found for the disease so that no more children would die and the need for transplants would diminish. I wondered would this be my last night ever looking at the little girl who had gone through so much but always considered herself a very lucky girl.

At 4.30 a.m. the phone at the nurses' station rang and Brigid, the Irish nurse answered it. She said, "Oh, it was positive, I'll pass it on." I did not realise the conversation affected us.

Finally I tore myself away from Gillian, kissed her gently on the top of the head and went back to bed. She slept with her eyes open as she usually did, which people found strange but we were used to it. I smiled as I left and said to myself, "I hope this is not my last night with you pet."

Too soon the alarm went off as I was two hours into my night's sleep. Coming back from the bathroom I met Brigid Conway and she looked worried, I just thought she was tired at the end of a long night. She told me Ian Martin wanted to speak to Brendan and myself. I thought it was to go over the schedule for the morning. When I was sitting on my bed still in my nightdress, and Brendan was halfway through brushing his teeth, Ian walked in looking concerned, and announced, "I'm sorry, the operation is cancelled. It can't go ahead." Brendan looked at him in amazement, with toothpaste still around his mouth. I just stared at Ian and said, "I don't believe it, why?" As I said this, for an instant I felt relief that we would not have to face it that day and immediately the relief disappeared to be replaced by the thought, "It's still all ahead in the future, it's just all too much". I felt in that moment I couldn't take any more stress in my life.

Quickly I pulled myself together afraid that Ian would think we couldn't handle things and it might jeopardise Gillian getting another chance at a later date. I was already thinking ahead as I usually did. Brendan didn't try to conceal his annoyance, in fact at a later date Mary Goodwin told me Brendan was angry when this happened.

Ian explained that the final test on the donor showed a positive cycomegalin virus which Gillian would inherit if the operation went ahead and this could cause serious problems. I asked him if they couldn't have taken a chance and he said, "It's difficult enough for it to work when everything is alright. To start off after such an operation fighting a virus in the new lungs which her body is not used to, would make it an impossible task. Would you put a faulty part in your car and think it was going to work properly?"

We knew it all made sense but we were just so disappointed. Ian and the whole transplant team were also disappointed. Everything had been set up for the operation. Logically we knew the team were experts and we had full confidence in their ability to make this decision. Emotionally it was very difficult for us. The thought of facing home and starting the wait all over again on the wretched bleep just seemed inconceivable. We knew this could happen, but you always think your luck has to change sometime.

Ian left and said he would see us later. Immediately I used the phone at the desk to phone Una to tell her, and ask her to tell Kelli and my parents. Una herself answered the phone. "It's all off, it's cancelled." "I don't believe it, what happened?" I told her briefly and said I would phone later to fill her in with the details of our return home.

It was considered keeping us in London for a few days but Dr Denham in Dublin said no, we should return to Dublin immediately. We were thankful for that as we were in no state to stay around that hospital.

Around 8.00 a.m. Gillian herself woke up and walked into our room, rubbing her eyes as she was still very sleepy. She didn't really react when we told her the operation was cancelled. I think she was a little relieved. She asked if we could go to Trafalgar Square and see the pigeons. It was like a reprieve to her. We had breakfast in the first place we came to up the road from the hospital. Brendan kept saying, "What rotten awful bad luck, I just don't believe it." My reaction was, "Well it's happened and it's just one of those things, we'll have to accept it." I felt absolutely exhausted, it had been a dreadful twenty-four hours and I just wanted to sleep.

We booked our flight for 9.20 p.m. after negotiating the use of an Irish cheque and we were to see a few people in the hospital in the afternoon. For Gillian's sake we decided to take her out for the morning. The effort of going out that day around London and trying to keep up a front was horrific. I just wanted to sleep for a week. We set off for Trafalgar Square in a taxi and spent some time feeding the pigeons, she was delighted. Afterwards we went down by the river at Charing Cross. We sat on a river boat for an hour or so, drinking coke and observing the busy bustle of the river Thames on this sunny Tuesday in June. By lunch time we had accepted we could not change anything and began to get philosophical and think perhaps there was a reason and maybe it was all for the best in the end. Maybe it was better they discovered the virus before rather than after the transplant. After lunch we made our way back to the hospital. There was a man's clothes shop near the hospital running a sale that day, so Brendan bought himself three lovely silk ties for a pound each. I thought to myself, "He's getting back to himself again".

Mr John Wallwork, our friend the surgeon from Papworth, was in the hospital that day. He came up briefly to say hello to Gillian. Dr Smith who we also knew from Papworth and Mr de Leval, the surgeon who was ready that morning to do the transplant, were with him. Gillian ran up to John Wallwork and gave him a big hug. We exchanged pleasantries and were introduced to Mr de Leval, whom we had never met before. They just said they hoped to see us back again soon. Gillian said afterwards how much she liked Mr Wallwork and that he wore the same aftershave as her Dad.

Mary Goodwin also came up and casually lay across the bed chatting. I think she wanted to see how we were handling things. She noticed Brendan's new ties and picked them up . "I see you were shopping." I asked Mary how many times this had happened, transplants being cancelled, and what was the eventual outcome. She said it had happened to three other children for different reasons. One had eventually received a transplant later, one had died and one was still waiting. So, statistically we were none the wiser as to what would happen to us. It was back to the bleep and the waiting game. Physiotherapy, nebulizer and Harcourt Street Hospital, and the uncertainty.

Ian came down to say goodbye and ordered a hospital car to take us to the airport. He put his arm around me and said, "Hang in there." He kept saying, "It's too bad." As we were waiting for the car in the lobby, Brendan remarked, "Isn't it a fact Ian, we could be just home and not even unpacked and we could get the call again."

"Yes, that could happen, for your sake I hope it does." He looked at Brendan in a funny way. So Brendan said, "On the other hand, it could be another year."

"Yes, that could happen also."

Our overall impression was that Ian Martin was disillusioned and he felt very sorry for us and felt we had come a long way for nothing. Of course Ian had seen this happen before.

When we checked in at the Aer Lingus desk at Heathrow you should have seen the look on the face of the chap working for Aer Lingus, who delivered us to the ambulance not twenty-four hours before. He asked what happened. He felt sorry for us and wished us the best of luck.

We relaxed on the plane and since things hadn't worked out we were glad we were getting home quickly. Deep in thought, Brendan suddenly said, "I wonder if that was our chance at it and it didn't work." I replied, "Don't think like that. We only waited three months, it could happen again within the next three months. Let's call it our trial run."

Kelli and Una were at the Airport and no-one could really believe what had happened. We arrived home very late. There was the bleep on the kitchen table, all ready to be carried everywhere again! Little did we know what was ahead. We seriously wondered under what circumstances we would finally return the bleep.

# 12. Kelli-Ann – A Victim

Gillian was physically the victim of cystic fibrosis but we all became its victims because it ruled our daily lives to such an extent. As the years went by and Gillian became sicker, it took over our lives completely in spite of our efforts in the early years not to let this happen. We knew it was happening but we were powerless to do anything about it.

Every day began with Gillian retching, coughing, and vomiting to get up the phlegm before she could breathe for another day. Even before the physiotherapy she went through this ritual. It didn't bother her because she had been enduring it ever since she could remember. Once it was over she would smile and say, "I love you Mum." She never complained. Brendan and myself never got used to watching our young child begin each day in this manner. Kelli never spoke about it, she just looked and listened and I think switched off.

After a cup of tea Gillian would go on her nebulizer with Ventolin to open her tubes, and antibiotics to treat the constant infection. This procedure was followed by half an hour of physiotherapy, holding her in various positions to clear the four sections of the lungs. On a week-day Kelli and myself would depart for school. Brendan would prepare Gillian's breakfast which was difficult for him as she was rarely hungry. He found it very frustrating because he knew how important it was for her to eat, both to fight the infection and at least maintain her already low weight.

There was always tension at meal times. Brendan said afterwards, the worst part of cystic fibrosis was trying to feed someone who wasn't interested in food. Brendan would then give Gillian about ten pills, the four Creon to digest and break down fats, oral antibiotics for infection and vitamins, in liquid and tablets for her nutritional status. Finally Brendan would depart to open his shop at 10 o'clock.

As time went by, we began to realise how much Gillian's illness had affected Kelli's life. We realised how difficult it had been for her to grow up in a house where there was constant sickness. Other people noticed even in the early years, but we were so busy trying to make sure Gillian survived we didn't notice. Dr Doyle would always say, "How is Kelli?" I suspect she knew from her experience of sickness that it would have to affect her.

Una took a great interest in Kelli from the beginning. In September 1983, one year after Gillian was diagnosed and was beginning to deteriorate, Kelli changed school once again to St. Patrick's and went into Una's first class. Una noticed she was very musical and creative, but lacked concentration and seemed to be in a world of her own. The report which came from her previous school said, "Kelli is a very intelligent little girl who is working well below her capacity at all times."

This was to be the type of report which would follow Kelli through her primary school years. She was calm, easy-going and dreamy and seemingly switched off most of the time in school. Always very pleasant and polite and well-behaved, she slid by without drawing too much attention to herself.

It's difficult to say how much Gillian's illness contributed to Kelli's lack of performance in school. I would say a combination of factors, including the illness and all that went with it.

In the early years, I felt she was a little immature and would achieve more as she developed. I don't believe in pressurising young children and creating barriers and blocks to learning. Intelligence will surface in the end, if it's there, and self-motivation is the only thing that works. So, Kelli skimmed by and anyway she always had the excuse that Gillian was sick, for things not being done. She was in the hospital late or at her

Grandmother's and forgot the books and so on and so forth. She learnt to read and write and acquired all the basic skills in spite of her apathy, but she did not develop good work patterns and was quite undisciplined regarding school work.

After teaching all day, coming home to physiotherapy and cooking dinner, to be honest I couldn't bear to look at a book to start forcing Kelli to do homework. As time went by, and Gillian became sicker and spent so much time in hospital, Kelli's school work was the last thing on our mind, "She has her health", Brendan would comment.

However, Una began teaching Kelli the recorder when she was about six and soon she was playing it very well. She also sang well and seemed to love music. On Saturday mornings both children went to Irish dancing classes and Kelli became a very good dancer. So it seemed Kelli's talents lay in music. At one stage Una began a school orchestra and Kelli was in it playing the recorder. Then Una, who is a lovely violinist, started teaching a group of children the violin and of course Kelli-Ann was one of them.

Ever since the children were very young we always had music nights in the house on Saturday or Sunday evening. By this I mean they would both perform for Brendan and myself. Gillian had a nice voice but was always too breathless to hit the higher notes. It used to break our hearts watching her trying to get the notes and knowing what was holding her back. They would make up modern dances and both perform, in later years imitating Michael Jackson. Gillian was a great little modern dancer up until the last year of her illness. Kelli would play the recorder and later the flute. When they weren't performing for us we were all listening to Frank Sinatra, Tony Bennett and Shirley Bassey, all great favourites of Brendan. We all have lovely memories of our music nights.

When Kelli was nine, Una said to me, "Veronica, the violin is not Kelli's instrument. I think she would be good on the flute." We began Kelli with flute lessons the September of her ninth birthday. She loved the flute from day one, and by Christmas was playing tunes and displaying a very nice sound. All this happened the winter I thought Gillian would never get off the couch again!

Kelli finally seemed to have found her thing in life and proclaimed her desire to be a "famous flautist". We were all amused. However, a year later she said, "Mrs Doris Keogh in the Royal Irish academy is the best teacher in Ireland and she is going to teach me." I have already described the circumstances of the audition, the same day Dr Denham informed us of Gillian's acceptance on the assessment list for the transplant.

The next event I will describe caused both Brendan and myself, especially Brendan, a lot of sadness. When Mrs Keogh decided to teach Kelli the flute in January 1988 she was completely unaware there was a huge problem in our house. She didn't know when she took Kelli out of two hundred applications, that Kelli had a little sister of seven who was very sick and hoping to have a heart and lung transplant in England. In addition she didn't know a lot of other things about Kelli-Ann and her music. In fact, we didn't know some of the things she was going to find out as time went by. What Mrs Keogh saw the day she auditioned Kelli was a little chubby ten-year-old with curly hair and big blue eyes who told her she wanted to be a famous flautist. In addition, she played the flute at Grade Three level with a lovely sound and displayed a very good ear in the ear tests. Mrs Keogh presumed she played so well from disciplined hard work and that her theory of music would be at the same level as her playing. She was wrong!

Kelli had not had theory lessons at all. She played well purely because of her natural talent for music. This was inherited from her father, who played the accordion by ear from the radio when he was three years of age.

Kelli was absolutely delighted she had succeeded in becoming a pupil of Doris Keogh's and kept telling everyone her teacher had taught James Galway. Poor Kelli thought that as long as she could continue making a nice sound with her flute she would succeed. She knew nothing about hours of good practice to improve technique – studying theory of music and reading difficult music in time. Mrs Keogh didn't know what Kelli was really like, and we didn't realise how absolutely single-minded she was about the flute. The relationship was fraught with problems and doomed to fail from the outset.

It was an enormous effort for us to get Kelli into the Academy every week for the flute lesson. We would go in straight after school. Kelli had to have a group theory lesson after Mrs Keogh's lesson and while this was going on Gillian was at home with my father, waiting for me to come home and do her physiotherapy. At exactly the time Kelli began with Mrs Keogh, I was on the brink of my negotiations on finance for the forthcoming assessment with the Cystic Fibrosis Association and the Eastern Health Board. The pressure on me was almost unbearable. The stress level was so high there were days I thought I would collapse. Sometimes it was to Harcourt Street Hospital we went to after the lesson, to see Gillian if she was in there.

Mrs Keogh wanted me to sit in on the lesson and take notes. I was very tired after teaching all day and very pre-occupied with worry about Gillian's assessment and health. In addition, her music language meant little to me. Brendan would have been good for this assignment but he couldn't leave the business.

When we went to London in April for the first assessment, Kelli told Mrs Keogh about Gillian needing a new heart and lungs. She knew then we had problems. After that my Dad would often take Kelli into the lesson and I would come straight home to Gillian. The schedule was very tight and any deviation caused problems. I

would ask Kelli how the lessons were going and she would say everything was fine. However, Brendan said to me one day, "Kelli seems to be spending an awful lot of time on the same few pieces."
For the first time I began to notice that Kelli was nervous every Thursday, before the flute lesson. I imagine this was the first time in her life she felt under pressure. The teachers in school understood she was living through a difficult situation, and I had told everyone to do their best with Kelli but not to pressurise her too much. I always felt in those early years to pressurise Kelli too much would cause more problems than it would solve. She wasn't great at school work, but in the circumstances, if she could remain happy and relaxed and not worry too much about Gillian it was all we wanted. We lived for each other for today, and tried to enjoy the times when Gillian was well and not in hospital. Our values were slightly different than other people who had healthy children.

For the last music lesson in June, Gillian and myself went along with Kelli. I knew that day Kelli was struggling, it was obvious she was out of her depth and yet I couldn't ascertain exactly why. Mrs Keogh kept saying, "Relax Kelli, what are you afraid of?" She kept stopping Kelli to correct mistakes and Kelli just seemed to get more and more uptight and aggravated. I thought it might be because it was the end of the school year and everyone was very tired. Mrs Keogh seemed to be covering a lot of ground in the lesson, and knowing Kelli I couldn't imagine her being able to comprehend and absorb everything she was saying.

Mrs Keogh certainly seemed to like Kelli but it crossed my mind that perhaps it wasn't going to work out. However, in the September of 1988, Kelli was accepted into the Junior Orchestra in the Academy, and as well as the Thursday lesson she went in on Saturday for Orchestra and several other activities. At this point I told Kelli she would have to start going in and out on the train by herself. The Academy was just down the road from the station. She played in a concert with the Orchestra at Christmas and Brendan and myself were very happy for her. But she just didn't seem to have the same confidence and self-assurance as all the other children. She looked lost and unsure of herself.

We felt sad for Kelli, because deep down we knew she was very musical but had not had the chance the other children in the Academy had because of the sickness she had grown up with. Nothing was said and we carried on hoping for the best for Kelli and Gillian. I felt that if Kelli could hang in long enough, and things were sorted out for Gillian, then automatically life for Kelli would get easier and she might begin to reach her potential.

Kelli's 5th class teacher, Bernadette Murphy told me that Kelli was working and doing quite well in school that year, but from the 3rd March 1989 when Kelli heard that Gillian had about a year to live, and was on the active list for transplantation, she switched off again and that was the end of progress in school. She went onto another planet, Bernadette said she saw the change overnight.

In the Royal Irish Academy they had external assessments every year and if you didn't get above 70% you couldn't continue as a student. In May we were delighted when Kelli got 89% in her assessment and told us she got the highest mark in her age group. Mrs Keogh was putting her forward for the Junior Scholarship. In spite of this Mrs Keogh asked Brendan and myself to go into a lesson in mid-June. She seemed confused by Kelli and there was something none of us could put our finger on. We watched the lesson and saw the same tension and apprehension on Kelli's part, as the previous year. Her counting seemed to be a problem and when Mrs Keogh explained it seemed to mean little to Kelli, she just looked blankly at her. But she had a lovely sound! We felt Mrs Keogh wanted to tell us something but she didn't. Something didn't add up, 89% in the assessment but there just seemed to be something not coming together. The following week we went to London for the transplant and it was cancelled as you have already read in the last chapter. Needless to say I never really thought much about Kelli's music that summer after our "Trial Run".

In September, Kelli was all set to win the Junior Scholarship. Apparently it was usually a pupil of Mrs Keogh's who won it. However, a requirement was for the pupil to have passed Grade One theory. No-one knew how weak Kelli was in this area. She had her first flute lesson of the year followed by her group theory lesson. The teacher gave her a sample theory paper to do and return it on the Saturday. She was supposed to sit the theory exam in the first week of October and the Scholarship later in October. Kelli did the theory paper on the train on Saturday morning and made a mess of it.

Mrs Keogh decided she could no longer teach Kelli the flute. Brendan received a phone call from her on Tuesday morning. She said Kelli couldn't do the scholarship because she had failed the mock theory paper and she had let her down badly. She said that Kelli was a lovely child and she was very fond of her but she hadn't made the grade. It boiled down to the fact that Kelli wasn't the calibre she wanted.

We were bitterly disappointed, Brendan especially took this very hard. He phoned me in school and said, "Doris Keogh has dropped Kelli". He was emotional about this, and other than Gillian's problem, I never saw him take anything as hard. He really felt Kelli had lost a fabulous opportunity, which of course she had and he blamed cystic fibrosis. We were very vulnerable and easily hurt at this particular time. It looked as if nothing could go right for us. Brendan felt life was not fair and of course it's not. However, normally we would not have reacted as strongly, but then in normal circumstances this wouldn't have happened because we would have kept a closer eye on the whole thing from day one.

Kelli initially was very upset but it was tinged with relief. The pressure was off but the little confidence she had was gone. She told us that when she started learning the flute in Bray she soon discovered that if the teacher played the piece she could play it by ear without reading the music. She got into this habit and in the end was playing everything by ear and never learnt to count or read music properly. This is where the problem lay with Doris Keogh. The missing piece of the jig-saw now fitted into place.

Within a few weeks Kelli was having private theory lessons and the teacher was asked to pay special attention to counting. She had a new flute teacher and was slowly regaining her confidence. Maybe it was all for the best, but still we couldn't help having some regret for what could have been for our beautiful eldest daughter, who is certainly very musical.

They say there is always a reason for things happening the way they do. Perhaps that is so!

*Kelli and Gillian (May 1990)*

# 13. Running Out of Time

At least our "Trial Run" reassured us that Gillian was indeed being seriously considered for transplantation. On the other hand, we now knew too much about the awful tension-filled hours prior to such an operation. The thought of going through the night I had spent in Great Ormond Street Hospital, looking at Gillian asleep, and wondering would it be her last night on this earth again made me feel sick. It had been hell for us emotionally from the time we received the call at 4.30 p.m., 26th June, until we arrived home twenty-four hours later.

We had to face it all again, and more, if Gillian was lucky enough to ever receive another call. However, knowing as much as we do about life, we knew it would never be exactly the same a second time. I hoped and prayed that if we were called again there would be no waiting overnight. It was too long to wait and still have to face the operation, there was too much time to think. Brendan and myself talked about what had happened over and over until we got it out of our system. Gillian, true to her usual self said, "Well, I feel that there is still some time for me and maybe I can enjoy the summer and get the transplant during the winter when the weather is bad anyway." She was putting a brave face on and trying to make the best of everything as she always did.

Everyone said how terrible it was to have come so close, but only ourselves knew how awful it really was. It was truly a traumatic experience. We thought about the donor family who had tried to help Gillian through their own tragedy.

Carolyn from Belfast was still waiting and Gwen, her Mum, and myself were in touch regularly. They were now waiting six months and thought it was an awful long time. If only they had known what was ahead of them. We were also in touch with Jo Hatton whom we had met in Papworth and who was four years over her transplant. Jo was a great source of inspiration to Gillian. She truthfully told Gillian how it really was. Jo wrote lovely letters encouraging Gillian to hang in and fight hard until organs were found. She said, "When you go on that list, your part of the bargain is to keep yourself as well as possible, stay alive until they can deliver their operation". Jo also told Gillian, "It's not easy before, during or after a transplant. Life will remain very difficult but worthwhile. You'll feel awful when you wake up after the operation and you'll have to fight your way back to life one day at a time." Gillian appreciated Jo's words of wisdom and advice and truthfulness.

We soon settled down to our normal routine of looking after Gillian and now I was on summer holidays I thought things would be a little easier. It should have been a summer whereby I rested and gathered enough energy to resume work in September, and wait for whatever lay ahead for Gillian. However, a lot of that summer of 1989 was spent in confrontation with the Eastern Health Board over money. The person dealing with our case was, I thought, cold, arrogant at times, rude and insensitive. On one occasion when I disagreed with the level of help offered towards expenses, I was told she would have to hang up the phone on me. There were arguments on the phone, long delays in answering letters, and the matter took four months and Dr O'Hanlon, the Minister for Health's intervention to resolve. I insisted it was not our fault we had to go out of the country to try and save Gillian's life and I was not accepting a cart with three wheels. I couldn't believe I had to use my dwindling energy to fight so hard over money.

During that summer we had a visit for a few days from Steven Brice, the twenty-three year old cystic whom we had met fifteen months before in Papworth, just after his transplant. Steven was from Bristol and we were looking forward to seeing a bouncing, energetic, post-transplant patient. He told us on the phone his quality of life was great now.

To be honest we were a little disillusioned about transplants when Steven left. He was still quite thin, ate very little, walked slowly, seemed tired and took lots of medication. However, he assured us he was in great form and felt well. We expected him to be much livelier. After much discussion we decided perhaps it was his personality. Also Steven had a job and had been working in the Television licence office in Bristol. So, perhaps he was tired, and I suppose it was an achievement to be back working within fifteen months of such major surgery.

Maybe our expectations of transplantation were unrealistic. One conjures up images of people and things, often the reality is different. As Jo Hatton said, "Everyone's recovery and progress is different. Some people progress steadily and slowly and continue to do well, and others do well with a speedy recovery initially and then suddenly things can go wrong dramatically."

We decided not to compare Gillian with anyone else. Brendan felt very confident that if Gillian got the operation she would "bounce back quickly and do very well". I was afraid to think that far ahead. The more I thought about the reality of what we were trying to do, the more I realised the enormity of the whole thing. It had seemed easy to say the words "heart and lung transplant". Brendan was hopeful and looking forward to Gillian getting the chance of it. I was wishing for time to stand still and not to lose her and not have to do anything. After the "trial run", I just panicked every time I thought about it. I felt insecure in my ability to survive what was expected of us.

Of course, being so busy trying to keep Gillian well took most of our waking hours. Gillian herself didn't talk much about the transplant until the summer was over and I was back at school in September. I began the school year 1989-90 feeling there would be drastic changes before the following September.

The days and weeks went by and still no call. Brendan and myself were going off to sleep late one Saturday night when the bleep went off. Initially I got a fright but almost immediately knew they would use the phone first. It was late at night and the phone was free so although I phoned, I knew it was a mistake.

We returned to Papworth in October for Gillian's six month review. She was deteriorating slowly. We knew at any time the slow deterioration could change and she could take a big jump downhill quite suddenly. I felt strange going back to Papworth but still not for the transplant. We had by now, made four trips to England. I thought about the previous trip when we had gone on the list and how hopeful Gwen and myself had been. Gwen's Carolyn was now waiting nine months, feeling sure it would happen soon.

As Christmas approached, we began to get worried that time was passing and we were slowly running out of it for Gillian. Every time she went into hospital for IV treatment, Brendan would say when the treatment was over, "Well, surely this is the last treatment, we will get the transplant before the next admission." But weeks later we would be back again. By Christmas we were nine months on the active list. We knew that children had died after being on the list for only three to six months. I was in constant touch by phone with Great Ormond Street. I usually spoke to either Ian Martin or Mary Goodwin. At one stage Gillian was the fifth longest on the list, then fourth, then third. By mid-December she was the second longest on the list and there had only been one heart and lung transplant in months. We drew our own conclusions and really became anxious. It looked as if the criteria of about a year of life left was pretty accurate. Some children didn't even get the year. We hoped and prayed we would be lucky.

We knew that Christmas 1989 would be our last Christmas together unless Gillian got her transplant. Gillian said she would love a big pink racer bike. I looked at her and she read my thoughts, because she responded to my look by saying, "I know Mum, I won't get much use out of it now, but it will be mine and I'll be looking forward to riding it after my transplant." What could any mother or father say to those words of wisdom and hope?

The problem was, Kelli had already asked for a bike and we had said we couldn't afford it. We were really put on the spot. Straight away Kelli said, "I asked first and you couldn't afford it, but now Gillian wants the same thing you couldn't afford for me and she's getting it and she can't even ride it because she has no breath." Gillian herself responded before we could try to explain, she said, "Kel, this will be my last Christmas if I don't get my transplant. I just want to have a pink racer, you have plenty of time to get one." That was that, Kelli gave her a hug and said, "Okay, don't worry Gillian you'll hang on until they get you organs, you're a fighter." It was said quite matter of factly and we could see our attitude, and outlook, and ability to speak about everything coming through in the children.

We enjoyed Christmas as usual and didn't dare let ourselves think seriously about the possible changes in the coming year. The pink bike sat in our hallway, shining and new and waiting to be used. The usual music nights took place but now Gillian became very breathless, very quickly, when she tried to dance. Brendan and myself relaxed and went for long walks on Bray beach. No matter what we talked about the conversation always came back to "Will Gillian get the call?"

Sometimes we felt confident she would and other times we had mixed feelings. Would Gill see her tenth birthday on 27th May, and if so, how would her health be by then if she didn't get the operation? If the doctors were accurate she would be living on borrowed time long before her birthday.

In January 1990, Susan O'Connell, a friend and colleague said to me, "Veronica, would you not consider going public, and doing an appeal for organs. You never know what might come out of it." I think Una also mentioned it. Marian Gavin told me they did an appeal and received the call about three weeks later. They were waiting three months altogether. Marian said they never knew if their appeal had any bearing on the fact that the transplant came up three weeks later. Margaret McStay told me if we decided to go public to let her know. Margaret and Marian often phoned, or I often phoned them just to chat. Both of these people knew exactly what we were going through because they had both gone through it for Jamie and Colin. Their support was very much appreciated.

We thought carefully about whether we should do a public appeal for organs. We asked Gillian how she felt. Gillian said she would like to give it the year on the list which would be the 3rd of March, see what happened and re-think it then. Soon after Christmas Gillian became the longest patient on the list in Great Ormond Street and still there had been no heart and lung transplants. We had been told that about 30% of children died while on the waiting list.

In February, Mary Goodwin told me they had transplanted a teenage boy with a new heart and lung and he was doing fine. We were delighted. During all these months there had been quite a few heart transplants. It was the double organs that seemed to be in short supply.

Ian Martin had explained already that they received offers of organs every week but the lungs were sometimes infected, damaged or just not the right size for any of their patients. Carolyn was still waiting patiently in Belfast and was very ill at this time. She had been in intensive care for many weeks all over

Christmas. Gwen and Harry thought they were losing her but she somehow hung in and finally came out of intensive care. It had all started with a bad flu which Carolyn picked up the night of her 21st birthday party in November.

I spent more and more time talking to Gillian very late at night after her physiotherapy. The few months after Christmas were extra special. We had recovered from the "trial run" and a sort of calm resignation came over us. We had done everything and now we had to be patient. There was no contact with the Health Board and so, many of the tensions of the assessments and negotiating the operation were gone. I found it a peaceful time. I savoured every minute spent with Gillian, each day was precious.

Gillian was still having private teaching two days a week with her teacher, Mary Walsh. However, Mary knew she was really not up to a lot of work at this stage, so Mary read a lot to her and did what she could. Gillian tired very, very easily. It must have been very frustrating for Mary to try and teach a very sick child. However, Mary persevered and had great patience with Gillian. Sometimes Gillian would just fall asleep during the lesson and Mary would just sit with her. Gillian told me one night she would worry about her academic skills if and when she got her transplant. "If I don't get the transplant I'm not going to be around to worry about maths", she commented.

She had good basic skills in reading and writing, very good natural oral language skills. Her maths wouldn't have been as good but we weren't worried. The rest of the time she watched a lot of television with my Dad, who stayed with her the two days the teacher didn't come. On a Monday Brendan was home. This was the day Gillian loved. Brendan usually took her out for a ride in the car and to a coffee shop. Sometimes they went for a walk on the beach, usually Brendan carrying her most of the way. Lucy the little dog went along sometimes and was a great source of joy to

Gillian. At this point there was no more walking to the shop which is about five minutes walk from our house. Gillian didn't say anything but I had noticed as time went by, she just didn't go to the shop any more because she wasn't up to the walk. The odd time she went it took her a long time to get there and back. It was sad to look at the new pink bike which was not being used and there was a big question mark as to whether Gillian would ever use it.

In February, as we approached the year on the list and still no call, we thought once more about doing an appeal. All our thoughts focussed on Gillian getting her transplant, nothing else was important any more. I continued to teach every day although I knew these were possibly Gillian's final months of life. It would have been lovely to have stayed home with her but it just wasn't possible. Brendan didn't go out until ten and came back at 1 o'clock until 2 o'clock and I came home at 3 o'clock. So it really was a very short few hours I was away from her. Gillian looked at me one day in February and said, "Listen Mum, I'm fed up waiting for that call to come. I want you to take me to get some nice photographs taken and send them into a modelling agency and I might get an ad. It would be lovely to do something different. This way I'd be waiting for something else besides the call."

We went and had the photos taken. They were lovely photos but, to be honest, her illness showed through in them. There was the face of a beautiful dying child staring at us from the photos. She went into hospital and the photos were never sent anywhere. Gill was beginning to get frustrated, "Why won't anyone donate for me Mum, there are accidents everyday and it's very sad, but it's more sad that the organs are wasted."

I told her people were donating but it was a matter of getting a match for her.

"Well, not enough people are donating or children wouldn't be dying on the list every day", she said.

"Maybe so, but it's hard for people who are not in the position to really understand the whole thing. If they haven't thought about transplantation ahead of a tragedy, it's very difficult for them to respond positively in their own darkest hour."

Gillian agreed with this and said, "Well maybe we should do an appeal for organs and even if I don't get it from the appeal, people will think and it might help someone else."

Brendan agreed that although it was unlikely we would get suitable organs as a direct result of an appeal, it was better than sitting by doing nothing. He said, "Maybe our appeal will get organs for someone else and maybe someone else's appeal in England will get organs for Gillian. It will also make everyone more aware of the need to carry donor cards and at least, think about the whole thing. It's worth trying anything at this stage."

So around the 10th March, one week after Gillian was a year on the list, I phoned Margaret McStay and told her we wanted to do a public appeal and how would we go about it. Margaret phoned me back a few days later and said, "Veronica, George Devlin from R.T.E. is going to do your appeal on the 6 o'clock television news, one day this week so be ready for a call."

George and his television crew arrived at the house at 1 p.m. on 16th March. I did an interview with them in our television room and they filmed me doing physiotherapy on Gillian. Then Gillian sat on the purple bean bag and did a short interview and told George how she hoped to be able to go down town and ride her bike if she got a transplant. We then moved into the kitchen and the whole family was filmed eating lunch. Brendan was going to stay in the shop for lunch when he heard what was happening, but I told him he had to come home because they wanted to film the whole family. As they filmed, I moved around the table flashing our ancient grey teapot while the two girls ate ham sandwiches.

Brendan sat straight up holding the side of the table and looked like a statue.

The ordeal was soon over and George and his team left, saying the appeal would go out on television that evening at 6 o'clock and they hoped Gillian would get her transplant. They were very nice. Brendan was five minutes back at work and I was recovering with a cup of coffee when the phone rang and Brendan said, "Ron, there's a gentleman here from the Inland Revenue. I told him you do the books so will you talk to him."

Apparently I hadn't sent in the P.35 form for the girl Brendan had working for him in the shop. I explained to this gentleman about Gillian and said I would have the form sent in within a week. He was very nice and said it was okay. "Phew, what a day", I said to myself. "Television crews and tax men, what next."

We watched ourselves on television that night and hoped it would do some good. It was all very emotional.

Next morning, St. Patrick's Day, we awoke to the sound of the phone ringing at 9 o'clock. It was a reporter from the *Evening Press* called Siobhan O'Neill from Bray and she wanted a story about Gillian for the paper. Siobhan couldn't understand how a child in Bray could be waiting for over a year for a heart and lung transplant and she hadn't heard about it. A photographer came out and took photos of us all. In the paper that night Gillian was beaming and Kelli looked as if it was herself who needed the transplant. This was how our public appeal began.

Within a week of the appeal for organs, Gillian returned to hospital with an infection and still no call. We wondered would she survive the infection. Marian Gavin phoned me one afternoon while Gillian was in hospital and said, "Veronica, we've just come back from Harefield, Jamie was over for a check up and do you know they have four or five children who have had transplants in the last few weeks. Would you consider trying to get Gillian on their list as well as Great Ormond Street and Papworth?" She continued, "I spoke to Jo Rae the Psychologist there and told her all about Gillian and how long you have been waiting. She said if you are interested, to phone her and have a chat."

It seemed very complicated to start getting involved with another hospital, however we were running out of time fast and were desperate . I phoned Jo Rae in Harefield immediately and she was really lovely. Jo said she had spoken to Dr Radley Smith, one of their consultants. Dr Radley Smith had said they would be delighted to get Gillian over within weeks for assessment as long as Great Ormond Street didn't mind, and Dr Denham would refer her and send all Gillian's medical history. The next day I phoned Mary Goodwin and said straight out "Mary, would you mind if we put Gillian on Harefield's list as well as yours." Mary seemed a little surprised but was very understanding. She knew how anxious we were as Gillian was the longest on their list now for three months. "Veronica, can I call you back in an hour or two when I've spoken to some of the team?"

Mary Goodwin called me back and said they had no objection to Gillian going on Harefield's list. She said the important thing was that Gillian got her transplant. They were all truly wonderful and understanding. Immediately I wrote to Dr Denham and asked if he could once again help us by referring Gillian to Harefield. I explained our position, and although we knew there were no guarantees, it would be an extra chance for Gillian and if everything failed we would feel no stone had been left unturned. He was great and did as I asked immediately. As Brendan said, "It would be our final hope." Now we just had to wait for a date from Harefield. We had waited thirteen months on Great Ormond Street's list and we really felt if she got a transplant it would be from Harefield.

From the outset, we knew it was the right decision to go public. We immediately felt we were doing something positive. Emotionally we were well able to handle it and that was what we had worried about. All the papers ran the appeal, but Siobhan O'Neill was great and did everything she could to keep the appeal going in the *Evening Press.* Siobhan made arrangements for Pat Kenny to interview myself and Gillian on his radio show.

On the morning of 18th April, Gillian and myself sat quietly inside the lobby of the radio station at R.T.E. waiting for Pat Kenny, who I think is Ireland's version of Terry Wogan.

A tall slim man with fair hair and glasses walked up the steps of the building. "It's Pat Kenny", I said to Gill. Pat immediately came over to us and shook our hands warmly. He went to take off his coat and came back a few minutes later. As we walked down to the studio with Pat we conversed easily. He kept looking at Gillian as she chatted about wanting to be a model when she grew up. Pat seemed impressed by Gillian the minute he set eyes on her. He really was extremely nice to us. We went into the studio, myself sitting opposite Pat. All of us had microphones in front of us. "Don't worry", Pat said, "it's not live, we can go over it if there are mistakes."

I thought the whole thing would only last a few minutes but not so. Pat started firing the questions at me about cystic fibrosis and went right back to the start of Gillian's problems. The interview went on for a long while. It went well first time. I think the high point of the whole thing was when Pat asked Gillian if she had anything to say to the public. She replied, "If death comes to your family, please think about donating. It is important to me and to other children." Pat also asked Gillian how it felt to be living on borrowed time. She responded, "I try not to think about it. It is one day at a time and I try to make the most of every day." When she was asked how she felt about facing the actual operation she said "I'm not afraid, it's something the doctors are doing every day."

Listening to Gillian speaking, it was hard to believe she was only nine years of age. Pat Kenny just kept looking at her. When the interview was over Pat took us for coffee and Gillian told him she watched his Saturday night television programme every week. They talked about the night he had the page three girls on. One would think it was two adults talking. When it was time to go Pat said he would like to show Gillian to the people of Ireland now that they had heard her. We agreed to come into his television show in a week or two if we hadn't gone for the operation.

The next morning our radio alarm woke us with the 8 o'clock news which began, "A thirteen-year-old girl from New Ross, Co. Wexford, Siobhan Anglim received a heart and lung transplant in Harefield Hospital, Middlesex last night".

Many people who heard about Siobhan's operation thought initially it was Gillian. We were delighted for the Anglim family and later read in the paper that Siobhan had suffered from a heart disorder since she was a baby. This was only Ireland's third heart and lung transplant. We hoped Gillian would be the fourth and the first cystic fibrosis victim.

"Mum?" "Yes Gill", I replied as I looked at Gillian standing in the doorway between the kitchen and living room. She still looked pretty although very thin, dressed in a blue green jumper and blue jeans. It was the day after she had appealed for organs on the Pat Kenny radio show. "Well," she continued, "I don't want to upset you, but just in case I don't get organs in time for myself, I want to donate any of my own organs that are okay. Will you arrange that for me?" I just hugged her close and said, "Of course," and she carried on. "My heart must go to England as I've promised it there, but my kidneys, liver and eyes could be used here in Ireland and, of course, my lungs are no good to anyone",

and she laughed. "It won't happen but just in case I don't make it." She was gone off to lie on her bean bag and watch television.
Gillian's breathing at this stage was getting faster by the day and we were very, very worried. However, she was beginning to enjoy all the publicity and she was looking forward to going on the Pat Kenny television show. This motivation was great for her because it gave her something to hang on for and take her mind off the reality of the situation. She found it all very exciting. It would have been lovely if the reason she was going on television had been different.
Gillian said she was absolutely determined to stay alive until organs could be found. She slept with a letter of encouragement from Jo Hatton, to fight to the bitter end, under her pillow and a signed photo of Pat Kenny by her bedside which read.

*Gillian, good luck with the op.*
*Love,*
*Pat Kenny*

On Saturday 28th April, the television cameras closed in on Gillian's beautiful little face and she held the attention of the whole country for several seconds. Once again Gill told Pat she didn't worry about borrowed time but lived and enjoyed each day. They talked of her hope to donate her own healthy heart when she had her transplant. When asked what she wanted to be when she grew up Gillian replied. "I'd like to be a model." I asked the public to think about the whole question of organ donation when things are going well, and before a tragedy strikes and try to understand the benefit to children like Gillian. Then I showed Pat the bleep we had been living with for the previous fourteen months. His concluding comments were, "Gillian is quite the bravest person I have met in a long time and if I had a choice between winning the Lotto tonight and that bleep going off, I would wish for the bleep to go off for Gillian."

Gillian was absolutely delighted. It was a very special evening. She was even more delighted when Olwyn Greene of "Sadie Greene Promotions" phoned the programme and said they were doing a modelling show in "Jury's Hotel" on Monday and would Gillian like to be a model for the night. It was a dream come true. They invited Gillian into Dublin on Monday morning to Clery's Department Store to pick outfits to model. However, I told Olwyn, Gillian wouldn't be up to going into Dublin during the day and then do the show that night. So they sent out some outfits from the measurements we gave them.

Gillian lay on her purple bean bag all day Sunday after the television show and again all day Monday and by 6 o'clock Monday evening she had conserved enough energy to do the modelling. I have never seen her as happy in all my life. Everyone made a big fuss of her. The models were all busy but they took time out for Gill. One well known model in particular, Brenda Hyland was really lovely. The press took lots of photos and it all made Gillian more determined than ever to hang on. She had so much to live for. The *Evening Herald* gave their whole page three next day to photos of Gillian modelling, and a lovely article entitled: "Gorgeous Gillian Star of the Catwalk."

The previous week our local T.D. (or Government Representative), Dick Roche had asked me if he would arrange for Gillian to go into the Dáil (or House of Parliament) to meet the Minister for Health to heighten donor awareness. So, two days after the modelling show Gillian had another exciting day. She had lots of photos taken on the lawn outside the Dáil with Dr Rory O'Hanlon, the Minister for Health. The Minister praised Gillian, especially her courage and sense of humour. Dick took us into the Dáil to meet Mr Charles Haughey, the Taoiseach (or Prime

Minister). Mr Haughey wished Gillian all the best of luck and invited her to come back and have ice-cream with him after the transplant. Gillian thought he was very nice. She said afterwards, "I hope we have the ice-cream together, actually I'd prefer burger and chips."

It was now 2nd May and Kelli was due to make her Confirmation on 12th May. We wondered if we would be gone for the transplant or to Harefield, on the day of the Confirmation. Kelli was worried she would have to make it without us. The 12th dawned bright and sunny and Kelli had her big day. After the ceremony my parents and brother Ian joined us for a meal in a hotel in Dun Laoghaire.

During the Confirmation meal, a lady came over to our table. She said she recognised Gillian from the Pat Kenny television show and wanted to wish us the best of luck. "It must be awful living like that waiting for it, how do you all keep going?" she said.

I didn't tell her that at this point it often crossed my mind how we actually did keep going with such a weight over our heads. But when you have no other choice what do you do? Instead I replied, "We just take each day and do our best to stay as normal as possible and it's the hope that we will eventually get the call that gives us the strength to keep going."

She told us that a year before her brother had lost a child in an accident. She said that when the child had died and they were about to turn off the machine, the doctors asked if they could use the organs for transplants. Her brother and family had refused because they were too upset. But afterwards, just a few days later, they changed their minds and were very sorry they had said no, but, of course, it was too late. She said as the months went by, they felt very sad they had refused.

This had been my point when we did the appeals. People must have already thought about these things before a tragedy occurs.

It is no time to start thinking about something as complex as organ donation when it is sprung on you for the first time at the worst possible time of your life. Especially if it's a child who has been lost. It's almost impossible for anyone to consider thinking about anyone else at such a devastating time.

After the Confirmation day, we began to get ready for our trip to Harefield Hospital, Middlesex, which was scheduled for Wednesday 23rd May. We just couldn't comprehend we were setting off to England for yet another assessment after already waiting fourteen months and a false alarm behind us. It really was a "Final Hope" mission.

The night before we left for Harefield, Kelli answered the phone and came into the kitchen, "Gill, there is a man on the phone wants to speak to you." I thought it was a reporter because the papers had been calling a lot around that time. However, I heard Gillian say, "Oh, hello Pat, I'm fine thanks." She had a good chat with Pat Kenny, the radio and television presenter and she was delighted he had taken the trouble to ring her. "He's really very nice you know", she commented as she went to sleep that night.

*My parents, Brendan, Kelli, Gillian and myself at Kelli's Confirmation (May 1990)*

# *14. Final Hope – Harefield*

The 23rd May was a beautiful sunny day as we set off on our fifth trip to London to our third hospital, in desperation trying to save Gillian's life. This really was our final hope. It was grasping at straws, but it was a chance and we were going for it. Gillian herself was in good spirits. As I said before, the hope of all the publicity had stimulated and motivated her to feel someone somewhere would donate and it would be right for her, and she would get her chance.

She knew how hard we had fought to get her this far and she also knew that going to Harefield was leaving no stone unturned for her. If there is such a thing as love keeping someone alive, Gillian Staunton was one such person. Gillian was not afraid to die, but she desperately wanted to live, and she knew how desperately we wanted her to live. It really was so sad to watch her going downhill and not be able to do anything but wait and hope every day for the call that could change things around for her. I often thought of the many cystics who never had this hope!

I had said to Brendan a few weeks before, that if Gill wasn't going to survive and do well after the transplant then I would prefer she didn't get it at all. He said, "No Ron, you would feel very frustrated after all the waiting. At least if something goes wrong afterwards, we will know she got her chance at it, and that would be easier to accept. Not to get it now would be dreadful after all your initial negotiating and all the assessments. You pioneered it for all the other cystic children in Southern Ireland and Gillian deserves to get a chance at it. There would have been no talk of transplants for cystics if you hadn't paved the way. "

It was all true, but I knew life was funny. I had worked hard for Gillian, and in so doing maybe I had opened up transplantation for other Irish children with her disease, but this didn't necessarily mean Gillian would get it if it wasn't meant to be.

Anyway, we arrived in the little village of Harefield in Middlesex, quite close to Heathrow Airport, at about 7 p.m. and booked into the one hotel in the place. Now we were all set to go down the road to the hospital early in the morning. We were not worried about the assessment which was only a matter of form and we were well used to the routine of the hospitals. I wouldn't have been up to this trip on my own and was very glad Brendan was with me. Once again Kelli was left behind to go to school and try to be as normal as possible.

Harefield Hospital could be compared to a mixture of Papworth and Great Ormond Street. It was set in a rural-type setting, with lots of grounds and a lake just like Papworth, but it had a children's wing and this reminded me of Great Ormond Street. There were brightly coloured walls and pictures, and equipment for children including a computer. As in the other two hospitals, everyone we met was extremely kind and just very nice. Jo Rae was a lovely girl.

We were in a brightly coloured ward with a little girl from Tyrone who was being assessed for a heart transplant and a little boy from India who was about to have corrective heart surgery. The whole family seemed to be there with him, mother, father, uncle and other relatives. They had all travelled from Calcutta to London for this operation.

The atmosphere around Harefield was very relaxed and people sat around outside the building on a patio drinking tea and chatting. We met quite a few people in those few days, all of us in the same position in one way or another. We all had very sick children, either waiting for corrective surgery or transplants, or coping with the post-transplant situation and what that brings. It's all another world entirely to what most people ever experience. On our first day there, we saw a few Irish-looking children running in and out of the garden.

"They must be the Anglim family", I said to Brendan. "Do you remember the little girl from Wexford who had the transplant on 18th April, the day we did the Pat Kenny radio appeal?"

It was the Anglim family. They had moved the whole family over and they had rented accommodation in the village. They were a really lovely family. Monica and John and their other five daughters had decided their best chance would be to have the family all together close to Siobhan. Unfortunately, that particular week Siobhan was not well. She had caught a virus within weeks of the transplant and was re-ventilated. They were very worried. It was a very difficult situation for these people. Like ourselves they had and were still, fighting very hard for their little girl and trying to look after their other children.

We agreed it was almost impossible having to go out of Ireland for this surgery. Gillian spent a lot of time talking to Fiona Anglim, who was around the same age as our Kelli.

"Fiona is very like Kelli", said Gillian. "Maybe it's because she had lived with a sick sister all her life, she even sounds like Kelli", she continued.

We hoped and prayed that Siobhan would be able to fight the virus and make a good recovery. John was smiling by the Saturday and said she seemed to be much better and was off the life support machine. We were all delighted. Brendan and John's brother, P.J., talked a lot in the evenings. P.J. told Brendan how he came over from Ireland as much as possible to give John a bit of support. Himself and John went off to the dogs the odd night to take John's mind off things. Monica and myself talked about how difficult the whole thing had been for all of us. We both agreed it was all a long shot, but at the end of the day, whatever happened, we would know we had fought and done our best for Siobhan and Gillian. They had only waited three weeks for the transplant.

John said, "You'll get it quick here, they go all over Europe for organs". This gave us new hope.

It was nice for Gillian to meet other children who had succeeded in getting their operation. Two young boys were walking around the wards both looking well. Lee Brash was fourteen and like Gillian has cystic fibrosis. He had received his new heart and lungs a month previously and had given his heart to Christopher Smith also fourteen, from Birmingham, who had an enlarged heart. The two boys were in adjoining rooms in Harefield and had become good friends. Both were doing well and it was great to see them. Lee's parents told us they had waited almost two years and when the transplant came they had almost given up hope. This was all good news to our ears,

I heard Lee joking with Christopher one day, "I'll take my heart back if you don't watch out". The two boy's rooms were covered in get well cards. I longed to see Gillian's room looking like theirs.

Lee showed Gillian how to use the computer and she spent hours and hours enjoying herself with "Batman".

Mikala was a blond smiling fourteen-year-old cystic fibrosis child who had come from Germany, and was now five weeks over her transplant. Mikala's parents had little or no English. When Brendan would see Mikala coming in and out of the hospital, he would give her Dad the thumbs up sign, and the German man would return the sign and smile. They were truly delighted their daughter was doing well. However, on our third day there, Mikala was rushed through the ward on a trolley, and when her Dad saw Brendan he immediately gave him the thumbs down sign and looked very sad. It was obviously not too serious because next day she was up and about again and it was thumbs up all around. We thought we were badly off but imagined trying to live through a transplant without a good knowledge of English.

Brendan and myself slept in a chalet-type building in the grounds of the hospital. It was very quiet and peaceful. We certainly felt we now knew a lot about British transplants and hospitals. Harefield and Papworth were the two major centres and Great Ormond Street had a small programme which was only in its second year, and had worked closely with Papworth in the initial stages. It certainly had been a very interesting experience for us.

Dr Radley Smith came to see Gillian on the third evening. She was a very busy, middle-aged, well-built lady whom we had spotted rushing in and out all week. She said to Gillian, "We are going to put you on our list and try and get you transplanted as soon as possible. It will be a race between us and Great Ormond Street to see who gets you first." Gillian laughed and we thanked her very much. It was all much less formal than Papworth and even a little more casual than Great Ormond Street.

That evening Brendan and myself went out to eat leaving Gillian busy at the computer. I told Brendan I felt that if Gill got the transplant it would probably be in Harefield. He just said, "I don't know, but I think she will get it very soon". We felt satisfied and were glad we had made the effort to get her to Harefield, thanks to Marian Gavin's kindness in thinking about Gillian.

We left Harefield early on Sunday morning 27th May, Gillian's 10th birthday. As we drove out of the village in a taxi, Brendan looked back and said, "It's a nice little village but somehow it reminds me of a little place we might never see again. I still think it will be Great Ormond Street." I don't know why he thought that, perhaps because Jo Rae had said, "You know Great Ormond Street are very committed to Gillian."

We knew that was true, and we were very grateful to the three hospitals in England that had shown great interest and dedication to our little girl.

We had exchanged phone numbers with John and Monica Anglim and hoped they would all soon return home with Siobhan. Their parting words to us were that they hoped we would be back with Gillian for the transplant very soon. When we arrived home that day Una had left a big birthday cake with ten candles and a big bottle of coke on our kitchen table. This was typical of Una.

*Gillian with Dr Rory O'Hanlon (May 1990)*

# 15. The Call

"Veronica, is that your Brendan running in through the main entrance?", commented my colleague. We were on yard duty in the main playground. I was standing with my back to the main entrance talking to Maureen as we supervised the children. I didn't even turn around but said, "No, my Brendan doesn't run anywhere."

It was Tuesday 12th June, a nice bright sunny day. Gillian had been in Harcourt Street, being treated for yet another chest infection, since Sunday. Her breathing was getting faster by the day and we were in no doubt there was very little time left.

The previous evening Brendan and myself had been in to visit Gillian. The hospital and surrounding area was very quiet that particular evening. Gillian needed things from the shop, and as she was dressed we decided, as it was such a lovely sunny evening we would all go for the short walk through the alley opposite the hospital. One of the world cup matches was on that evening, hence the deserted streets. We walked very slowly to the shop as Gillian was quite breathless.

On our return we slowly approached the hospital, Gillian in between Brendan and myself holding a hand each. We stopped for a moment, all of us sensing a peace and quiet. A calmness came over us as we looked across at the hospital. We looked at the words "Harcourt Street Children's Hospital" in bold letters over the entrance. In that moment all three of us sensed something different, as if we knew it was the end of an era.

I said, "Isn't it a beautiful evening, it's so quiet". We reflected a moment longer and then proceeded across the road and back up to the ward. We kissed Gillian good-night as she sat on the bed with her legs crossed and her long dark hair flowing across her shoulders, still pretty although very thin. Little did we know the next time we would see her she would be sitting on another bed, in another hospital, in another country. "See you tomorrow night pet", we said as we left.

Later that night, when Brendan and Kelli had gone to bed and I was feeding the dog and locking up, I sat down and started to think about the recent visit to Harefield Hospital two weeks previously, and all the assessments we had been through. There had been five trips to hospitals in England and still no transplant. I knew if we didn't get the transplant very soon we wouldn't need it. I had all my hopes pinned on Harefield. That night I said. "Please God give her a chance. After all the waiting let her have the transplant and after that, I'll accept whatever is your will for her."

The next morning all that was forgotten and I switched off as usual from personal problems and went off to school.

Maureen suddenly said, "It is Brendan, Veronica, he's calling you."

"Something must be wrong", I said, and tore off up the steep tarmac towards him. He was waving his hands frantically and speaking but I was too far away to hear what he was saying. I thought maybe something was wrong with one of my parents, but as I got closer I heard, "Great Ormond Street Hospital". My tummy dropped, straight away I thought, "It will be cancelled again. I can't go through it again."

In contrast to the previous "call", I went to pieces and just kept saying, "I can't go through it again". As we entered the staff room Brendan said, "Pull yourself together, we've to pick Gillian up at Harcourt Street and get out to the airport by 5 o'clock." I flung the Principal's door open and interrupted a meeting with a priest. After causing chaos in the school for ten minutes we were on our way to the house to pack.

Brendan started telling me how he was going to go to Superquinn for chicken for his lunch, but decided to go straight home and use what was in the house.

"I was just opening a tin of sardines when the phone rang. I looked at the clock, it said 1 o'clock and I was sure it was Gillian as she never fails to ring me", said Brendan.

He said he got the shock of his life when a voice said, "Hello, Mr Staunton, this is Dr McCabe from Harcourt Street. We've had a call from Great Ormond Street and they have a potential donor for Gillian. Can you pick Gillian up and head out to the airport, you've to be there at 5 o'clock, the flight is already booked."

Obviously there was a misunderstanding because Brendan thought it was the airport for 5 o'clock, when in fact we were expected at Great Ormond Street by 5 o'clock. As a result we thought we had plenty of time and even intended going down to tell my parents before we left Bray. Una, Kelli, Brendan and myself and Ann Kelly, a colleague who had offered to drive us to the airport as Una didn't have the car, were pottering around the house packing cases, etc., myself still in a panic generally talking in circles. I decided to phone Harcourt Street to find out exactly what time our flight was leaving and to re-assure Gillian as I hadn't spoken to her at all.

When I got through to the Medical Ward I nearly died when the nurse said, "Where are you?"

"At home, we are leaving soon", I replied.

"Oh" she said, "we have all just waved Gillian off outside the hospital."

I knew then there had been a mistake. It was all stops out after that. A police escort was arranged and off we went on a "Starsky and Hutch" chase from Bray to Dublin Airport.

The squad car took us as far as Cabinteely. A neighbour of ours, Mick Mulcahy was one of the guards in the car. He, of course, knew Gillian well. He gave us a big wave with tears in his eyes as we continued on with the police bikes. Poor Ann was under dreadful pressure from Brendan, who was sitting beside her. She wasn't used to keeping up with specially trained guards on bikes, whizzing in and out of traffic.

Brendan kept saying, "Keep up with them or there is no point, no-one will know we are with them." Una, in the back of the car with Kelli and myself, said, "Leave her, she's doing fine."

By the time we arrived at the East Link bridge, Ann was quite an expert. We were flying along right behind the bikes. I had calmed down and blotted out the events we were going to face before we went to bed again. My philosophy has always been that life is always changing and that's what makes it interesting. Each day we awake, we don't really know what changes for the good or bad will take place before the day is over. Someone told me once, when I was a young student, I needed too much excitement in my life.

Well, 12th June 1990, I certainly got more of it than I could handle. Crossing the toll bridge and heading out to the airport road my mind flashed back to almost a year ago when we had crossed this bridge on the same mission. Una had driven us quietly to the airport without any fuss. That was all before going public and appealing for organs. We went, and came back the next day without anyone in the media even knowing. I always knew if we had another chance at it that things would be completely different. Gillian was in the car with us the last time and we knew we would have to wait all through the night, because the transplant wasn't scheduled until the following morning. It was too long. This time we knew it was sometime that evening, which I was glad about although we didn't have a clue what time and Gillian wasn't with us. As the airport came into view I began to get excited at the prospect of being re-united with Gillian. The Garda escort was fantastic, they took us from Bray to Dublin Airport in twenty minutes during a busy Tuesday afternoon.

Rushing into the departure terminal we headed for the B.E.A. desk, looking frantically around for Gillian. We couldn't see her anywhere. "She's gone", we were told. It was another disappointment. This confirmed our fears that surgery was scheduled early and now we might not even see our Gillian before she went to theatre. In fact, we might never see her again. It didn't bear thinking about.

"How was she?" I asked. "She was in good form and went off quite happily" was the reply. Typical of Gillian, putting on a brave front — she was a great kid.

The tickets were made out for us to go on the next flight which was an Aer Lingus flight. I said, "Please make the tickets yearly returns and give me an open return ticket for Gillian. We will all be home within six weeks." And we were. This was my eternal optimism shining through to the bitter end.

Immediately we had to leave, and once more say goodbye to our Kelli. Poor Kelli hadn't even said goodbye to Gillian. Everyone kept the front up. "Don't worry Kelli, everything will be fine. We'll phone you every day and let you know how things are and you can come over to see Gillian as soon as it's possible, probably next week", we told Kelli. We hugged Kelli, Una and Ann and took off for our flight.

"Don't forget to tell my Mum and Dad," were my last words to Una.

Once we were airborne we just looked at each other speechless. Brendan just said, "It's out of our hands now, we have absolutely no control over events. It's what we have waited and hoped, and prayed for, it's up to God now".

He shrugged his shoulders in resignation when I kept saying, "But we might not even see her before it and what must Gillian herself be feeling."

I thought back two days to our last meal at home. Gillian had looked at me across the dinner table and she said, "Mum, supposing I get the call while I'm in hospital and you and Dad don't make it to the airport in time, what would happen?"

I replied, "Gillian, that won't happen but if it did for some reason, you get yourself to London for that transplant, don't wait for anyone. Don't worry, we will be with you but you are the important one and just go ahead and we will follow." It was absolutely ironic that she should have asked that question, and then for it to happen. I hoped my reply had helped her cope that afternoon.

We spoke very little on that lonely journey from Dublin to London, but we silently communicated shared feelings of excitement, that Gillian would hopefully get another shot at life. Fear – of what could go wrong and how we would cope if it did. Sadness – that we were not with her and that the hugs we gave her the previous night in Harcourt Street might have been our last hugs forever. The knowledge that Gillian might have to face the ordeal of going to theatre without us by her side was almost too much to bear. We might have already said goodbye to her with the hugs and kisses the night before without knowing it. It's a situation that many people find themselves in every day of the week when there is a sudden accident. In fact, a situation the poor donor family had probably endured in recent days. We knew 10% died on the operating table.

We felt an element of relief as we flew to London. It was finally going one way or the other. Our long shot had come to pass and Gillian and all of us would have a much better quality of life if it worked. If it failed we would be spared the heartache of the very final stage of a child dying from cystic fibrosis. We had witnessed the final few weeks of this awful disease where the child is gasping dreadfully to draw each breath, depending on oxygen for relief every minute of every day until it is finally over.

Finally, having gone through the gamut of emotions we felt very grateful and thankful that through the miracle of medical science, the goodwill of this British hospital and the donor family, Gillian was going to get this fantastic chance we felt she truly deserved after her courageous and determined fight, during which she never lost her sense of humour, kindness and deep caring of other people. She had appreciated every day we had loved and cared for her. She knew we had put up a great fight to get her a transplant and now hopefully, if it were God's will, it would all come to pass. We could possibly enjoy in the future a phase in our life which had hitherto been unknown to us.

Minutes after our arrival in Terminal One at Heathrow, I tore off to the B.E.A. desk. They were very good and immediately put a call through to Great Ormond Street. "Could I please speak to Ian Martin." Minutes later, "Hello, can I help you, Bruce Whitehead speaking, Ian Martin isn't here".

"Hello Doctor, this is Veronica Staunton. We are at Heathrow and will be along immediately. What time is surgery scheduled for?"

"Hello Mrs. Staunton, relax it's at 8 o'clock." I heaved a sigh of relief and instantly realised Ian and the team had left to harvest the organs.

"Where is the donor from, is it a boy or girl?"

"It's a little boy from the North of England. Ian will tell you what you are supposed to know later."

I felt sad for the other people. "Will you tell Gillian to relax, that we will be there shortly."

"Of course, see you soon."

As we came through the arrivals lounge I saw a familiar looking man waiting for someone off the plane. I realised it was John Anglim. He was surprised to see me. I said, "John, we got the call, the transplant is tonight." We only had a minute to talk. He was delighted for us. John said he was waiting for his mother.

It was 5.45 p.m., and we were re-united with Gillian at 6.30 p.m. There she was, sitting on the bed with her legs crossed in her red silk blouse and blue denim boiler suit exactly as she had looked when we left Harcourt Street twenty-four hours before. This time she was busy taking off her nail polish, a requirement for the operation. She was absolutely delighted to see us and we were delighted to see her. For a minute in our excitement we forgot the schedule for the night. We explained to Gillian and Mary Goodwin what had happened regarding the mix-up about the airport.

Gillian said, "Yes, I knew there had been a mistake. Dr McCabe said one thing to Dad on the phone and something else when she got off the phone. I was in too much of a daze to correct her, but I knew it was all wrong."

It was the talk of the hospital how this little girl of ten had arrived from Ireland on her own for a heart and lung transplant. They were amazed at her composure and confidence. Gillian said when she arrived in the ambulance everyone she met said. "Where are your parents?"

"Oh they will be here soon, there was a bit of a mix-up."

After the initial excitement of being re-united we began again to think of what was ahead. Mary Goodwin went home for an hour to eat and come back at 7.30 p.m., by which time we thought we would be on the last lap and ready to go down to theatre.

The surgeon, Mr de Leval came up to see Gillian, a slender, fit looking man with glasses and a slight French accent. "I think we have good lungs for you this time Gillian", he said. But it still wasn't definite. The team were at the donor hospital and would not know for certain if the lungs were alright until they were extracted.

There was a delay at the donor hospital and so our surgery was going to be later than planned. It was going to be a long night. Gillian was given her first dose of Cyclosporin, the anti-rejection drug in anticipation of the surgery going ahead. We just sat around chatting for several hours.

# 16. Gillian's Account of Events 12-13 June 1990

I woke up in the middle of the night in my hospital bed in Harcourt Street. There were nurses and ambulance men in the small ward. I looked across the ward and saw my friend gasping for breath. The nurse told me her lungs had collapsed. I was very upset so they moved Trevor and myself out into the corridor and put us back in when we were asleep. The curtains were pulled around my friend all of the next day. I could hear her asking her Mum to help her, she couldn't breath and I got very upset. At lunch time they moved me out into another ward and I never saw my friend again. She died the following evening.

After lunch I was sitting on my bed when a nurse said I was going for an X-ray. I didn't want to bother because I was busy playing cards with Trevor. As I was coming back in the lift from X-ray I said to the nurse, "There is a strange atmosphere around here, there is something fishy going on."

As I came out of the lift Dr Denham picked me up and swung me around. He held me out in front of him and said, "Great Ormond Street is looking for you."

I felt nervous, happy, and sad all at once and my tummy turned over. Dr Denham said to the three students with him, "This is going to be Southern Ireland's first cystic heart and lung transplant patient." He looked happy for me and gave me a big hug and told me to call home.

Dr McCabe, the house doctor, phoned my Dad and told him the good news. Dad couldn't wait to get down to Mum's school to tell her and Kelli. When we got off the phone, I asked Dr McCabe about the arrangements and she told me something different to what she had told my Dad. I knew there was a mix- up but I was too muddled to try and sort it out. But I wasn't very surprised when Mum and Dad didn't arrive and me and Dr Denham and Bernie, the Sister, were waiting in the lobby for ages. Dr Denham said to me in the end, "Mum and Dad must have been held up. Will you go ahead on your own Gillian? We can't wait any longer." I said, "Do I have any choice?"

The next minute he gave Bernie a load of money and said, "Here's a few quid for an emergency." I knew then Bernie was coming with me. I had known her since I was a baby. She is lovely so I was happy she was coming. I felt like a zombie, everyone was talking and it was all going over my head. All I could think about was the night ahead and would it be another false alarm. I knew if it was a false alarm I wouldn't get another chance. There wouldn't be much more time for me.

Then Bernie and myself got into the police car and Dr Denham and some of the nurses waved me off from the front door of the hospital. He looked happy. I really missed my Mum and Dad and wondered when I would see them. Would they be at the airport and would Kelli be with them. I was very sad I had not said goodbye to my sister and Lucy my little dog. I really wondered if I would ever see any of them again.

On the way Bernie said, "Your Mum will be delighted for you Gill. I'm glad for her, you have all waited so long, it's a great chance."

When we got to the airport Bernie and myself looked around to see if Mum and Dad were there but they weren't. People from B.E.A. came up to us and started asking about forms. I didn't know what they were talking about. Bernie didn't seem to have enough money for an air ticket, she said to me privately, "Do you think the Eastern Health Board would pay for a ticket for me?" I laughed and said "I don't think so." Then the lady from B.E.A.

said they were sending one of their staff, a young fellow, over with me. I wanted Bernie to come but no-one offered to let her on the plane. They put me in a wheelchair and Bernie gave me a big hug goodbye. She had tears in her eyes and said, "See you soon Gill".
My big worry was would it be another false alarm because of what happened the first time I flew over, nearly a year before. On the plane I was very quiet, the chap they sent was very nice. I can't remember his name but he said, "when I woke up this morning I didn't think I would be going to London." I laughed. He kept talking to me but I wasn't listening. I just kept looking out the window thinking about the night ahead.
Another nice, older man from the crew called Don McLean took me up into the cockpit and let me work the controls. I put the plane left and then right. This was exciting and helped take my mind off things. When I left the plane Don shook my hand and said I was a great girl. I didn't feel very great. I felt very nervous and sick.
The ambulance was waiting for me and once again, they asked where were my parents. I just said they would be along later. All the way into London in the ambulance I kept worrying it would be a false alarm again. I also thought how great it would be for me if I got the transplant and things worked out. This thought made me very excited.
When we arrived in Great Ormond Street at 5.15 p.m. I met a lovely young nurse called Sharon who asked about Mum and Dad. They weighed me and put in a drip. I asked the doctor what time the transplant was starting and he said around 7.30 p.m. Then another doctor came in, he said he was Bruce Whitehead and he would be looking after me after the transplant. He said Mum and Dad were at Heathrow and were on their way. Then I started to relax.

When Mum and Dad arrived I gave them a big hug and Dad said, "We're finally here pet."

The worst part of the whole night was at 10.30 p.m. when we started to go down to theatre. For the first time in my life I felt completely alone. Mum and Dad couldn't help me. They couldn't go through this for me. When it was time for Mum and Dad to go I wanted to say, "No, I don't want it", but the thing that stopped me saying it, was the fact I didn't want any negative thoughts in my head going asleep. I wondered would I ever see my Mum and Dad again. When they pushed the trolley through the door and left Mum and Dad behind I felt horrible, as if I was in a nightmare. They were really going to open up my body and take out my heart and lungs. The only thing that helped me was knowing other people had gone through this and woken up to a new life.

Everyone had masks on and were dressed in green, like something out of Twilight Zone. Straight away a tall man came up to me with a big needle in his hand, with a syringe full of white milky liquid. As he was pushing the needle into the drip I asked was it the anaesthetic and before he could answer I was gone.

The next thing I remember was hearing voices, laughing and talking. One man's voice said, "I hate kids who sleep with their eyes open." They thought I was asleep and I felt frustrated. I could hear but couldn't move a bone in my body. I could just see light in front of me and thought I was still in theatre. I fell asleep again and when I woke again there was tape on my eyes.

I made a groaning noise and could move my fingers this time. They took the tape off my eyes and I was glad they knew I was awake. I sensed Dad there and he kissed my cheek. The next thing Mum was squeezing my hand and I knew the operation was over. I knew now nothing would stop me surviving.

# 17. The Transplant

At 10.30 p.m. Mary Goodwin came into the room where we had been waiting for four and a half hours and said it was time to go down to theatre. Brendan and myself stood one at each side of the trolley as it was wheeled along the corridor into the lift, and down to the first floor. Gillian remained cheerful throughout and we continued to chat to each other and Mary until we arrived at the theatre door. We entered a set of swing doors and immediately Bruce appeared dressed in green and masked up. He just said, "We're ready to get started."

Calmly and without emotion Gillian handed me her white and pink swatch watch and lovely little heart shaped gold ring with a tiny little sapphire, both presents from us two weeks previously for her tenth birthday. "Look after these Mum until tomorrow, don't lose them." Brendan and myself kissed her and calmly our eyes met for just a second. "We'll see you in the morning pet." In a flash she was gone, the trolley was pushed quickly through the second set of swing doors.

I have never felt so helpless in all my life and would gladly have changed places with Gill if I could. Not one tear was shed by any of us. Gillian was truly fantastic. I will never forget her courage as long as I live. I looked at the watch and little ring which would have fitted a four-year-old and placed them carefully in my pocket. I silently prayed, "God, please look after her and give her back to us."

Mary Goodwin invited us to have coffee in her room, we thanked her but said we hadn't eaten since breakfast and would go out for a meal. On the way out we phoned Una and told her it was under way. She said she would go down and tell my parents. Una said her phone hadn't stopped ringing all evening with people asking how things were. She said Kelli had spent the evening playing her flute. Brendan and myself walked into the first Italian restaurant we came across along Southampton Row. We ate a meal in almost silence. We were very afraid and nervous, but Brendan joked with the waiter. He looked up at a violin hanging high up on the wall and said, "Take it down and I'll play you a tune."

We were truly alone. A party of six people laughed and joked at the next table. Couples looked into each others eyes. We ate in stunned silence. It was going to be a long night and one we would remember for ever. We were a long way from home in a difficult situation. After the meal we returned to the hospital. Brendan went down to the basement where we would sleep for a few nights and I went up to the third floor where we had spent most of our time since arriving.

Bonham Carter Ward was becoming very familiar to me since the false alarm and the assessment. I passed the room where Gillian had been all evening, and on to the nurses' station where three nurses were laughing and joking. It was now almost midnight. One of the nurses asked me if she would call theatre and see how things were going. I said, "Yes please." When she put the phone down she said, "Yes, everything is going well. They started an hour ago and Gillian's own organs have been extracted and they are now waiting for the new ones to arrive." "You mean the organs are not here yet?" I responded. "No", she replied calmly. "They are due in about ten minutes."

I went back to Brendan and told him what the nurse had said. "Oh, my God", he responded and rolled over on the bed.

I phoned Margaret and Leonard McStay and told them Gillian was in theatre. They were delighted we had finally got our chance. We slept for a few hours.

Silence prevailed in the deserted corridor on the 1st floor of the hospital on that fateful night. It was now 3.00 a.m., 13th June, I stood silently outside the swing doors leading to theatre. The only sound was the ticking of the clock. Lost in my thoughts, I was just unable to comprehend what was happening beyond those swing doors, I so badly wanted confirmation that things were going well! But there was no-one around. I suppose I didn't really expect to see anyone around this particular corridor, at this time of the morning. If I had gone to the desk upstairs they would have phoned down to see what stage the operation was at. Subconsciously I had come here to be closer to Gillian. Staring at the swing doors I conjured up images of what was happening beyond.

We had lived, hoped, prayed and waited for this day for a long time. Heart and lung transplant had become very familiar words to us. I had spoken the words very casually for a long time. Now, as I stood there alone, panic set in, I had a great urge to scream out loudly, "No, no, no, give me my child back, it can't work!" I did nothing.

The operation was not expected to finish until 4.00 to 5.00 a.m. so I was just about to return to Brendan in the basement. Suddenly, a tall figure clad in green, masked up with only two brown eyes visible pushed his way through the swing doors. "It's over", he said. It was so early I thought something must be wrong. "Is she alright?" I asked. "Mr de Leval will explain", and he was gone.

I waited, a moment later the surgeon appeared, his eyes looked very tired. "I think it will be okay", he said with his slight French accent. I thought to myself, "He thinks, only thinks, it will be okay." Think wasn't good enough for me. He explained that during the operation there was a little problem with one of the lungs. The left base collapsed a little and wouldn't come up. However in the end it inflated on its own without any help. He said they would be bringing Gillian out in five minutes. I tore down to the basement to get Brendan.

In a flash Brendan jumped off the top of the bed, shoved his feet into the slippers and out the door. He had been asleep and I think the action of shoving his feet into the slippers indicated to me, he still thought he was home in Bray, in his own house.

We had barely embarked from the lift on the first floor when the doors marked "Theatre" swung open and a trolley was pushed through. We received our first glimpse of Gillian. It was like something out of a film. I've seen this scene many times on the screen. Figures clad in green everywhere, hats, masks – the lot. The figure on the trolley looked like a corpse, deadly white and wax like. There seemed to be tubes coming out of every part of her body.

Brendan and myself just watched the proceedings in a daze. Everything was blurred. We stood apart from the action as Gillian was wheeled into the lift. I only wanted to see her from a distance looking like this. At this point I just couldn't believe I would ever see her laughing and smiling again. We were invited into the lift but we spontaneously declined and said we would rather walk up. It was hard for us to identify with the corpse-like figure on the trolley. Ian Martin, the transplant co-ordinator and person who had gone to retrieve the organs, walked up the single flight of stairs to the second floor with us. Brendan tripped and nearly fell going up the stairs as one of the brown slippers fell off his foot.

In normal circumstances I would have laughed at the sight of him, his hair standing up straight, a shirt half opened and the famous brown slippers.

We sat on the blue couch outside the transplant suite. This was the special air-conditioned intensive care unit where Gillian was to spend the next two weeks. Ian said we could see Gillian in about fifteen minutes when she was set up in the suite.

Suddenly, I thought about the donor family and how they must be feeling. We still had hope, they had already lost everything and yet they had agreed to give our child a chance to live. I asked Ian what he could tell us about the donor. He said the donor was a nine-year-old boy who had died from head injuries received in an accident. He said the kidneys and liver had also been donated. So four people were getting a chance to live through their tragedy and generosity. Another doctor had already told me what part of England the donor came from. I asked Ian if it was a car accident. He hesitated and then said, "No, it was a very different kind of accident."

Ian looked very tired, it had been a hectic day for him. He is a nice, friendly, warm person and he tried to reassure us that it was a case of so far so good. At 4.00 a.m. Ian went home to grab a few hours sleep, shower and change and appear for work in the morning.

The transplant suite was a specially designed unit. There was a central control room with phones etc., in the centre, surrounded by three identical rooms where three transplant patients could be housed if necessary. One could view the patient through a large wide glass door. This door could be opened to bring in X-ray machines etc.

The normal entry to the air-conditioned inner room was through a tiny room to the side which housed a sink and all the mask-up gear. One entered the little room, washed one's hands and put on a hat, apron and mask and then opened another small door into the patient. The wash and mask-up procedure had to be carried out each time you came into the patient. If you went out to the control room to take a phone call you had to wash and re-mask up again to re-enter to the patient. This happened for the first four or five days.

Before Ian left, he took us into the control room where we looked through the wide glass door at our baby. The bed was length ways in front of us and Gillian looked as if she were laid out! Only the mass of machines indicated differently. "She won't wake up for a few hours yet, so why don't you get some sleep?" said one of the staff. Brendan and myself returned to our very hot room in the basement. We were told we would be phoned if there was a problem. I phoned Una to say she was out of theatre.

Dozed is the appropriate word for what we did for the next few hours. After 6 a.m. the phone outside our room never stopped ringing. There were about eight bedrooms in the basement, a little kitchen, sitting room, two toilets and two baths. Each time the phone rang we jumped, thinking it was bad news about Gillian, but each time another name was shouted out and a mother was asked to go up to her child.

At 7 a.m. I again viewed Gillian through the glass as she was still asleep. Her eyes were taped up. However the next time Brendan went up about 7.30 a.m. she was beginning to wake up. He went into the room and kissed her on the tiny piece of her cheek not covered in tubes. She knew he was there and reacted by shaking her head. He immediately came down and told me Gill was waking up. I washed my hands and masked up for the first time and entered the inner sanctuary.

Margaret McStay had said, "Veronica, no matter how many people you see in Intensive Care, nothing can prepare you for the shock when it's your own flesh and blood." She was right!

Brendan and myself stood either side of Gillian and just looked in horror. Her head was tilted back with the wide tube of the life support down her throat. Several tubes came from her neck. Four tubes came from the chest, two upper and two lower. This was the sight I found hard to adjust to, blood was pumping back and forth through these opaque tubes and the heart was visibly pumping up and down beneath the surface of the skin. It took a minute to absorb this.

We found it difficult to accept seeing Gillian in this situation. But, she was alive and awake! We held a hand each and she squeezed back. Brendan held his thumb and first finger of his right hand an inch apart and Gillian showed traces of a smile. This had been Brendan's prepared signal to her before the transplant. He would say, "Gillian, you will get a little better each day." He would hold his finger up and say, "You'll fight hard and we will be right there with you, fighting with you and little by little you will get better and be running around with your new heart and lungs ready to start a new life. Then you will know it was worth all the waiting and the fighting. Hang in."

I said, "Are you in pain pet?" and she shook her head. I noticed her lips were very dry but pink and asked if she would like some ice. She nodded. When I put small pieces of ice in her mouth she managed a little smile. After that she drifted back to sleep. Brendan and myself will never forget those first minutes of our child's second chance. It is difficult for the human mind to comprehend such happenings.

Brendan left first, and I stayed a minute longer just looking at the little girl we had brought into the world ten short years previously. It all became too much and as I took off the mask and apron I was visibly close to tears. Pauline, the Welsh nurse who was going to look after Gillian so well in the coming days asked me if I was okay.

We went in and out for short intervals for an hour or so. Finally we adjusted to the reality of Gillian and the tubes. Once I knew she wasn't in any pain it became easier. It was truly fantastic how they were able to keep her completely out of pain and so comfortable.

I phoned Una again at 8 o'clock to tell her Gill was awake. She was thrilled and said she'd go down to tell Mum and Dad before going to school. Kelli was happy.

Brendan and myself went out to eat breakfast about 9.00 a.m. I bought the *Daily Mail* and on the second page there it was, the story of the tragedy which led to Gillian's transplant. It described how the little nine-year-old boy had died and the heart, lungs, kidneys and liver had been donated for transplants. Although I knew we would never contact these people directly, it was nice to be able to put a name on the young child whose tragedy and family's generosity had made things possible for Gillian.

We had been told Gillian wouldn't be able to speak until the life support was out and it normally came out within twenty-four hours. However, Gillian managed to speak with it in. She told Pauline she wanted it out and wanted to breathe on her own. She nagged them all day and within ten hours of waking up she was breathing on her own!

The next few days passed in a daze and we hardly knew night from day. Drugs followed drugs and doctors came and went continuously. All sorts of flowers, telegrams, cards and letters arrived from all over Ireland. The Taoiseach, Charles Haughey sent a lovely basket of flowers. The Tanaiste, Brian Lenihan sent a telegram and phoned twice. He understood well, as he had undergone a liver transplant a year previously. Our local T.D., Dick Roche sent a telegram and made several phone calls.

We realised the significance of it all. Gillian had indeed made Irish medical history. She had become Southern Ireland's first cystic fibrosis heart and lung transplant patient. It had really happened! We truly appreciated all the messages of support and goodwill. It seemed as if all Ireland were rooting for Gillian. She had been a trooper and deserved all the attention. It was appreciated all the more because we were on our own, away from home.

Brendan answered the phone in the central room of the transplant suite the evening after the operation. A man's voice said he would like information about the wee girl who had come from Ireland the day before for a transplant. Brendan said he was Gillian's Dad and that she had come through the operation fine. He said his name was Don McLean and he worked for B.E.A. and had been one of the crew on the plane when Gillian came over the day before. He told Brendan he had never been as impressed with any child in his life. He said he thought about her all night. "She shook my hand and thanked me for letting her work the controls, and said goodbye as if she was going on her holidays. She was unbelievable."

Don gave Brendan his phone number and said he had a flat out near Heathrow and was away a lot, so to give him a ring if we needed accommodation any time. Brendan was touched by his kindness.

Ian Martin, Brendan and myself were having a chat during the first afternoon after the operation. We were in the control room of the transplant suite and Gillian was still in and out of sleep in the inner room with Pauline at her side.

I asked Ian if I could see Gillian's old lungs. Straight away Brendan said, "No Ron, you don't want to see them." "But I do want to see them," I insisted. Ian said, "Veronica, you can't see them because they have already gone off to be used for research, but we took photos of them and I'll let you see them in a week or two." I was disappointed but said, "Okay, but was there much good lung left?" "No, very little, they were awful."

A few weeks later Ian showed me a slide of Gillian's old lungs. There were a few tiny patches of good tissue left, each the size of a nail on the right lung. The left was completely gone. It's amazing how she was alive at all.

The nursing and medical care Gillian received in the transplant suite was superb. Bruce Whitehead, a lovely Australian, was the medical man in charge of Gillian. He was constantly in and out looking at the large chart pinned on the outside of the mask up room. Everything was monitored very closely. Mr de Leval, the surgeon was in and out all the time. But Pauline Whitmore, the Welsh nurse was the most professional nurse we had ever seen in action. She was absolutely fantastic. Brendan and myself agreed we would never forget the way Pauline looked after our Gillian the first five days after her operation. Pauline was efficient but she also mothered Gillian through and explained everything to her and answered all her questions. She reassured Gill and gave her lots of confidence, to get through those first crucial days.

Everything Gillian ate was completely sterile and came from a special section of the kitchen. Knives, forks and spoons were all wrapped separately. Little sachets of coffee, squares of butter and cheese and even slices of bread were individually wrapped. We brought in about ten cans of coke for her every day because once a can was opened she would use it to take her drugs and the rest would be thrown away within fifteen minutes.

It was so important that Gill didn't get a virus in those first days – hence all the precautions. Anyone with even a slight cold was not allowed into the transplant suite.

At night three lovely Irish nurses looked after her, Pam from Cork, Mary Moylan from Dublin and Fiona. It was like being at home with the girls and Gillian had good fun with them, talking late into the night. They were delighted to have an Irish child to nurse.

On the third night after the operation. Brendan and myself went out to eat. When we came back Gillian had a mobile telephone in the room and told us she had phoned Kelli and her friend Claire. Kelli thought it was someone playing a joke and got quite upset until Fiona went on the phone and assured her it was indeed Gillian. Tim Healy answered his phone and a voice said, "Can I speak to Claire please?" "Who's calling?" he asked. Gillian said, "When I said 'It's Gillian', the phone just went dead silent. He sounded surprised." Anyway after that there was no doubt back in Bray that Gillian was on the road to a speedy recovery.

All the tubes were out by day three and the next day, when we came back from lunch Pauline had Gillian dressed, and up on an exercise bike, pedaling away. She cycled so many kilometres every day. It was truly wonderful.

For the first time in ten years we let someone else look after Gill. We were still in a daze and Pauline was doing such a great job I took a break. We went in and out and let the medical staff get on with it. I heard Pauline rattling off a list of drugs and the very names overwhelmed me. I wasn't ready to tackle them at all.

On the Sunday evening Maggie and Ray came up and we went out for a drink with them. It was good to dress up and get away for an hour. They waved in at Gillian through the glass door and thought she looked great for what she had been through. Brendan hadn't seen Maggie and Ray since we had spent a weekend in London in 1977 when Kelli was a baby and before Gillian was born. A lot had happened to us in the intervening years.

The next morning I did a radio interview with Pat Kenny. I had to wait a few minutes on the open line for Pat to come on and could hear the programme. An argument was going on about Ireland and the World Cup. I realised how out of touch we were with everything, isolated. We were in another world. Next minute I heard Pat say, "Well now, on to some very good news. You will remember a while back we had a little girl, Gillian Staunton and her mother Veronica on the programme. Gillian needed a heart and lung transplant because her lungs were destroyed by cystic fibrosis. Well, happily last Tuesday night, Gillian had her transplant in Great Ormond Street Hospital in London and became Southern Ireland's first cystic fibrosis sufferer to receive such a transplant. Now we have Veronica on the line."

I think the interview went well and Pat invited Gillian and myself to go into the studio when we came home.

Two days later Gillian's X-ray was fuzzy, she had a complication and rejection was diagnosed. This was expected and almost always happens around day seven. It was treated and the X-ray cleared. This was the only time she has had symptoms of any rejection although we have seen hints of it in biopsies. John Wallwork, the surgeon from Papworth came in to see her that day, as did Virginia O'Brien. They were delighted for us all and John gave me a big hug. It had all begun with him in Papworth.

Kelli arrived on Thursday laden down with letters, tapes, posters and presents galore for Gillian. Aer Lingus had given Kelli a present of an air ticket at the request of Dick Roche, our T.D. Kelli just kept looking at Gillian in amazement. Gillian was the same old Gillian and they soon settled into their old relationship.

On Saturday Gillian took her first walk out of the hospital just ten days post-transplant. Photographers from the *Irish Independent* had waited for hours outside the hospital to take pictures. We all slowly walked to a little square nearby. She looked very pale but mustered up her old smile for the photographs. Kelli couldn't take her eyes off her young sister. She seemed fascinated that Gillian was up and walking around so soon after such an operation.

When we returned to the hospital we had a surprise visit from Monica and John Anglim. They said Siobhan was quite well but they still hadn't returned home to Ireland. John kept looking closely at Gillian who was swinging around in one of the swivel chairs in the centre room of the transplant suite. John commented, "She looks very well and she's so active for just ten days over that operation. Our Siobhan was never that strong after it." We had nothing to compare with, this was our only experience of seeing anyone ten days post-transplant. Gillian always took everything in her stride. I suppose it really was marvellous if you consider what had happened and that children can take a couple of weeks to get over an appendix operation.

Brendan and Kelli returned home to Bray on Sunday. It is a small business Brendan has and if he hadn't returned he would have lost it. We would like to have stayed together throughout the whole thing but longterm, it wouldn't have been wise. We decided they would both come back again in two weeks.

The following two weeks were awful for me. Gillian had her first lung biopsy the day after Brendan left. This was the only way of finding out if there was any rejection of the lungs. They put her to sleep and used a bronchoscope to look down at the lungs and snipped a little tissue to send to the laboratory to see if there was any rejection. She was very sick after that first biopsy and it just seemed as if the trauma would continue for ever. Then she had some good days.

My parents came for a few days and it was lovely to see them. They couldn't believe how quickly Gillian had recovered. We went to the park and she climbed up on slides and swings. My Mum said, "You wouldn't think there was a thing wrong with her. I can't believe it."

While my parents were there, Gill moved out of the transplant suite back up to Bonham Carter Ward. She was in a small room on her own. I phoned Brendan or he phoned me two or three times a day. This was our only way of giving each other the support we needed. It seemed as if we were well on our way now. However, there were days when she was still very sick from all the drugs. When the level of Cyclosporin, the anti-rejection drug, went too high she would vomit and feel awful. It was difficult to get the levels they wanted because Gillian still had cystic fibrosis in her digestive system and she wasn't absorbing the cyclosporin at the same rate all the time. This is an added complication for cystics with transplants.

Some days she would feel very sick and tired and not want to get up. I would say, "Come on Gill, get washed and dressed and we will go out for an hour or two and you'll feel better. You must make the effort to do things even if you don't feel great. You have to fight for it."

Within three weeks of the operation I had her out in the British Museum, at a musical and walking all over London. We went out for at least two or three hours every day. Then she felt she had achieved something for the day and allowed herself to rest and watch television the rest of the time in between laughing and joking with the doctors and nurses.

My Aunt May came from Coventry to see Gillian and was also amazed at her progress. It was nice to see her and I appreciated her kindness in making the effort to come down.

By this stage I was giving Gill all her drugs myself and ticking them all off, four times every day in the little blue book which she will use to record the drugs and her daily temperature for the rest of her life.

Another feature of each day was the use of the microspirometer which indicates how the lungs are working. It's a little grey machine with a mouth piece. Gill blows into it everyday and if the blow drops more than 20% it indicates a problem, possibly rejection.

I was sleeping in the basement in a room I shared with three other mothers. It was amazing how institutionalised one can become. The heat in London was almost unbearable at times and I longed for the cool fresh sea air of Bray.

During this time, Gillian met another little boy her own age called Trevor Glass, also a cystic child who had his transplant five weeks before Gillian. He was in for a few days to be treated for a chest infection and they were delighted to have each other to exchange experiences.

Trevor lived just outside London and was able to come in and out of Great Ormond Street easily whenever there was a little problem.

Another young girl from Ireland came over for an assessment in July. Young Orla Roche was lovely, she was thirteen and from Kilkenny. Her Mum, Una, was delighted to see Gillian running around and said they had seen Gillian on Pat Kenny before the transplant. She said, when they heard Gill had become the first cystic fibrosis patient to get it, they were delighted and it gave them hope for Orla. She was going to ask their consultant about it but he suggested it first and here she was for an assessment. When I heard Orla coughing all the time, it reminded me of Gillian a month earlier.

One morning Una Roche said to me, "Veronica, did you know that they only get five years out of a transplant?" I said, "They only say that because they are only doing them five years, but Una, Gillian didn't have five months left when she got it, so five years is a long time."

They put Orla on the provisional list and said they would reassess her in November. When I looked at Orla and Una I was very glad we were over the operation, whatever happened. Una asked me how long we waited. "Fifteen months on the active list but some people only wait a very short time. I hope Orla will be lucky," I replied. Gillian and Orla chatted animately. Gillian explained all about the transplant to her.

Once we were up on Bonham Carter Ward we saw less and less of the transplant team. Mr de Leval, the surgeon, would often come and just have a quick look at the chart on the window and go off. Gillian had been very lucky and had remained stable throughout. Apparently many things can go wrong especially in the first week or so. Some children have to be re-ventilated.

It was difficult to get Gillian's feeling about everything. When I would say, "Isn't it marvellous Gill." She would just laugh and nod her head. I was always trying to pin her down as to how she felt. "Well", she said, "I can breathe much more easily and it's great in between feeling very nauseous from the drugs. I still feel tired at times. Really I feel as if I've gone from one side of a wall to the other." I knew as time went by and she became stronger and more used to the drugs she would begin to slowly move away from the side of the wall!

Bruce told us we would move out of the hospital into the Sick Children's Trust house around the corner for a few weeks and come in every second day for Cyclosporin levels. This was the next step before returning home. In fact if we had lived closer, we could have returned home a month after the operation.

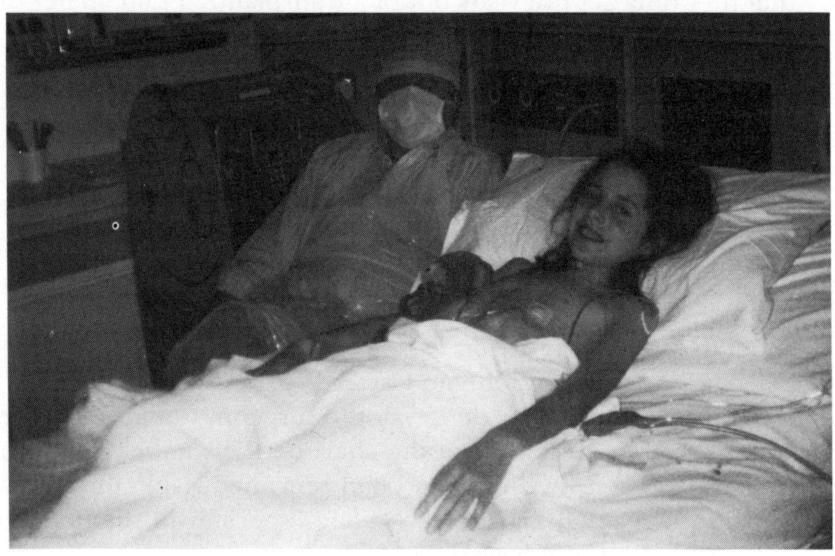

*Gillian and Brendan – second day post-operation*

# 18. Meeting a Duchess

She looked lovely, her long red hair shining and her blue eyes sparkling, and much slimmer than we imagined. A nice natural personality which I found refreshing. Her arms swinging by her side she strode into the kitchen and said, "Well, who have we got here?" Pat introduced Gillian and myself. "This is Gillian Staunton and her mother, Veronica, from Ireland. Gillian has cystic fibrosis and she has had a heart and lung transplant four weeks ago today. Isn't she looking great?" She shook my hand and Gillian's. "Hello Gillian," said her Royal Highness, The Duchess of York, "And how are you feeling?" Gillian beamed her best smile and said, "Hello Mam, I'm feeling great thank you."

"What sort of things are you able to do now that you couldn't do previously?" continued the Duchess.

"I can walk without getting breathless and I've more energy and now I'll be able to go back to school in September and ride my bike."

Her Royal Highness concluded, "Well Gillian, it's nice to see you looking so well and good luck for the future." She shook hands with Gillian and myself and she moved on to speak to the other families in the room.

This event took place on 11th July, three days after Gillian and myself moved out of the hospital into 10 Guildford Street, The Sick Children's Trust House, just around the corner from Great Ormond Street Hospital.

The Sick Children's Trust was founded by Dr Jon Pritchard and Professor James Malpas back in 1981. The idea behind it was to have a house near a children's hospital where the families of very sick children from far away could spend time as a family. The first house, Rainbow House, which is near Great Ormond Street Hospital was opened in 1984.

In 1985 Michael Crawford did an appeal on B.B.C. television. £154,000 was raised. A second house was bought near St. Bartholomew's Hospital. At this stage, more than 350 families had stayed in Rainbow House. Michael Crawford said, "The Sick Children's Trust is unique in being able to offer whole families help at this distressing time. Many families find it impossible to re-arrange their lives when treatment centres are a long way away. But surely no family should be forced apart when such a tragedy occurs? I think the home from home idea is a great opportunity to help solve that problem."

It was the third house, 10 Guildford Street, that Gillian and myself had moved into on Monday 9th July, just three and a half weeks after her transplant. The whole idea was great and the work being done by the Trust is really worthwhile.

Brendan had been over for the weekend, and on the Monday morning we came around to the house to meet Pat Percival, the manageress, and get a key. We sat down in Pat's office and she said, "The official opening of the house is on Wednesday. We have the Duchess of York coming, so I've to send the names and addresses of everyone staying in the house into Buckingham Palace for security reasons." So our names and address went off to the Palace! The last time my name went to the Palace was way back in 1962 when I became a Queen's Guide, the highest honour for a Girl Guide.

The house was really very comfortable. There was a lovely big television room with a huge television, and nice size fully fitted kitchen and laundry room. There was a bathroom off each of the first three floors. There were seven bedrooms. Pale blue carpeting ran throughout the house and beautiful drapes and furnishing had been donated by Marks & Spencers. This would be our home for the next few weeks. Brendan would stay at weekends when he came over.

I was really looking forward to a change from the hospital, although a little apprehensive about being on my own with Gillian without the security and support of the hospital staff. However, we would only be around the corner and we would go in every second day for Cyclosporic levels – a blood test to determine if the correct amount of the anti-rejection drug was being absorbed into the system.

Brendan helped us to move into Guildford Street before Kelli and himself went off on the bus for the airport. We left Gillian watching television in her new temporary home while I waved them off. As the bus pulled off towards the airport Kelli and Brendan blew kisses and waved, their faces got smaller and smaller and my tears bigger and bigger. I felt very sad, lonely and sorry for myself that Monday evening. The two previous weeks without Brendan had been very difficult for me. I allowed the tears to roll down my face as I walked the five minute walk back to Gillian. It didn't matter if people looked at me. I didn't care. It would be weeks before I would see Kelli as she couldn't come over again because it was too expensive. Then as I reached the house I had a little chat with myself and cheered up, "Stop your nonsense, you're on the down stretch now. Brendan will be back in a few days and you and Gillian will have a great rest in this nice house and enjoy being out of the hospital."

It's amazing, but we had become institutionalised and missed the hospital for a few days. Gillian missed having fun with the doctors and nurses, everyone loved her and she them. However, Gillian was looking forward to meeting a real live Duchess and a member of the Royal Family. She wanted to know why we didn't have a Royal Family in Ireland. She decided she would wear a dress for the special occasion, the dress she had worn when Brendan and herself had gone to the Frank Sinatra concert in Dublin the previous summer.

On Tuesday we slept late and relaxed. We spent a few hours in the park. The weather was brilliant, lovely beach weather, very very hot. Everytime I looked at Gillian she wanted a cold can of coke. Gillian slept for a few hours that afternoon, she still tired easily, not surprising after such major surgery. Pat kept introducing her to everyone and they were all amazed she looked so well and was so full of life and fun within the month. She climbed the five flights of stairs to our bedroom several times that day. I would say, "Gill, bring everything you need because I'll never make it back up again until I go to bed tonight."

I don't want to sound ungrateful to the hospital but it was terrific to be out of their basement and sleeping in nice surroundings again. Cyclosporin levels were due to be taken at 9 o'clock on Wednesday morning and then we had to get back to the house for the Royal visit. We had nice hot baths and went off to bed early. Pat was like a driven woman getting the house in order for the visitor the next day.

She was already flapping around when we left for the hospital at 8.30 a.m., she was seeing dust that wasn't there. Barbara and Lily, the two ladies who had part-time cleaning jobs in the house were dashing around. "Don't forget to be back before 10.30 a.m. Veronica," shouted Pat as we left. "The sniffer dogs are coming to do their security check then, and no-one will be allowed to enter or leave the house until after the Duchess leaves." "Don't worry, we'll be back in an hour or so", I replied.

We told Bruce to hurry up because we needed to get back to dickie up to meet the Duchess of York. At 9.30 a.m. we were finished in the hospital and went for breakfast to our regular little café close by. The sun was shining so we sat outside the café and read the morning papers while waiting for our food. By the time we returned to Guildford Street everything and everyone looked superb. I hardly knew Pat she looked so glamorous. Gillian looked at her pretty navy and white dress before putting it on and said, "Well, I must say I feel much better today than the last time I wore this dress Mum. Remember I wore it for Frankie, Sammy and Liza, and now today for a Princess, isn't it exciting. Hope it still fits me!" She giggled as I struggled to pull up the zip, it barely zipped up.

Gill thought the sniffer dogs were lovely as they sniffed their way through our bedroom. They were beautifully groomed and very well-trained dogs.

Pat asked us to go down and relax in the kitchen with a few other families. She asked one or two families to stay in their rooms and one or two to situate themselves in the television room. In this way the Duchess would meet people all over the house as she was escorted around by Pat and the two trustees.

The whole thing was very nice and Gillian was delighted she had finally met someone important in London. Everyone kept speaking in the hospital about this one, that one and the other coming to the hospital but we had missed them all.

It was a bit of an anti-climax when the Duchess left, so for a treat we took a taxi down to the Angus Steak House in Oxford Street and had a lunch of hamburgers, chips and coke. Afterwards we spent time looking in the less crowded shops in Oxford Street. We couldn't go on trains or buses or into any busy enclosed crowded places still because of the risk of infection. Since the operation Gillian was obliged to wear a mask in all public places. At this stage the mask had been discarded.

Later that day when Gillian was resting, one of the trustees knocked on our door and he told me there was a phone call in his office from the London office of the *Irish Independent* and asked if I would come down and take it. It was only then I discovered a suite on the first floor was used as offices for the trustee staff of the house.

From this office much of the fund-raising was initiated to maintain this beautiful home from home, where families with sick children could maintain some sort of normality. We were already benefiting from the great work of "The Sick Children's Trust." During our everyday lives we often subscribe to various charties without ever getting into the details of the work they do. Here we were benefitting from the hard work of the British public.

I told the reporter all about Gillian's meeting with the Duchess of York and how she was progressing in general, since the transplant. She said the story would be in the *Independent* in Ireland the next day. This comment made me homesick.

I phoned Ray and Maggie and they came up that evening with two of their children and we all sat in the garden of a nearby hotel and chatted for an hour or two. Cora and Niamh were company for Gillian and I enjoyed the chat. We gave them a conducted tour of our new home, they thought it was terrific accommodation. Ray and Maggie were great. They knew I wasn't always in form for company but when I was they were always willing to come up and go for a drink and a chat. It was nice to know they were there. On the weekends Brendan didn't come over, Ray would pick Gillian and myself up and take us out to their home for the day. Ray's Mum and Dad lived three doors down the road and they were amazed at Gillian's progress. I had known all the Stone family since my student days in London.

Brendan came over again on the Saturday evening and we enjoyed the weekend together. Gillian told him all about the Duchess of York and how she wore navy and white clothes, the same colours as Gillian's dress. He looked very tired because he had gone straight back to work within two weeks of the transplant. His first week back at work had been very stressful because he had left Gillian still in intensive care and every time the phone rang he was apprehensive. The whole trauma was beginning to show on him at this stage. At least I had nothing else to worry about every day apart from looking after Gillian. It seemed inconceivable to me to have to work in our present emotional state.

Brendan joined Gillian and myself in 10 Guildford Street for the weekend. Pat very kindly moved us into a bigger room for the days Brendan was over. Bruce told us if everything kept going well we could return home on Friday 27th July, that would be just over six weeks since our arrival. It was now 15th July and the only reason we hadn't gone home already was the fact that we were living out of the country. Gillian had made a marvellous recovery and remained very stable throughout. Some days she felt very sick and had bad headaches from all the drugs, but she never complained. I would know she wasn't well when she was very quiet. During the weekend of 15th July, I told Brendan not to bother coming over the next weekend as we would be home within days. He looked relieved. I knew he wasn't up to all the travelling. We both kept looking at Gillian and saying, "It's a miracle".

Now we felt we could relax a little and comment on the success of the whole thing. We knew it was still, and would always be, one day at a time. But things had gone well and hopefully with a little luck Gillian would now have some good quality life. She certainly deserved a good spell.

We were really looking forward to getting home and into our own house once again. Gillian couldn't wait to see Lucy her little dog, and all her friends, and of course Kelli. Brendan went off on the bus quite happy this time. In fact we were all happier because we felt we were on the down stretch and had come successfully through something enormous.

Because Brendan wasn't coming the next weekend Gillian and myself went down to the East Coast for the weekend, to stay with a very old school and college friend. Margaret and myself had gone through primary, secondary school and College together. She always used to joke about when I first arrived from Ireland back in the fifties. I wasn't familiar with the word spam, and I would say ,"I have to get some spum for my Mum."

Margaret and Mike lived in an old-world cottage in Rye with their two little boys, Sean, ten and Michael, three. The weather was beautiful that weekend and it was lovely to see Margaret. We stayed up talking until very late Friday evening. My greatest moment of joy and happiness since the operation came on the Saturday. Mike dropped Margaret, the two boys, Gillian and myself at the beach and said he would pick us up in the evening.

Margaret and myself sat on two chairs up on a height overlooking the beach. The mid-day sun beamed down on us, with just enough of a breeze to make it pleasant. Sean, Gillian and Michael clambered down the deep sandy slope to the water. While chatting away to Margaret and enjoying the peaceful beach my gaze wandered down towards the blue water. It was a moment I will remember as long as I live. Gillian was running along the edge of the water, her long dark hair blowing in the breeze and her laughter ringing throughout the beach. The two boys in close pursuit. Margaret followed my gaze and said, "Isn't it amazing?"

The final week went very quickly and soon it was time to say goodbye to all the lovely people we had met in the hospital and to Pat in the Trust House.

Everyone had been fantastic and although I would have liked to have had the transplant in Dublin, Great Ormond Street had been an experience I will remember forever.

I will conclude with a quote from "Mutual Friends" by Jules Kosky, which is very appropriate and I wholeheartly agree with.

*"Great Ormond Street is not only a place of medical excellence in the forefront of paediatric research and technique, it is also a symbol, a place of hope. It is this symbolic function that has in the end the most significance and the most meaning, the greatest appeal to the public who have given it*

*such unstinting support. It is a place where the spirit and the remarkable patience and bravery of the young still help the doctors and the nurses perform miracles. Great Ormond Street seems to the anguished mother her last chance to ward off the encroachment of death. Or if it does happen, alas that her child was in the right place, was in Great Ormond Street, and the gratitude that such bereaved parents often express has always been among the most tender and moving episodes of its history. This gives it a character of its own, different from the children's hospitals, no matter how wonderful they may be and are. It is a place for dreams as well as intensive care."*

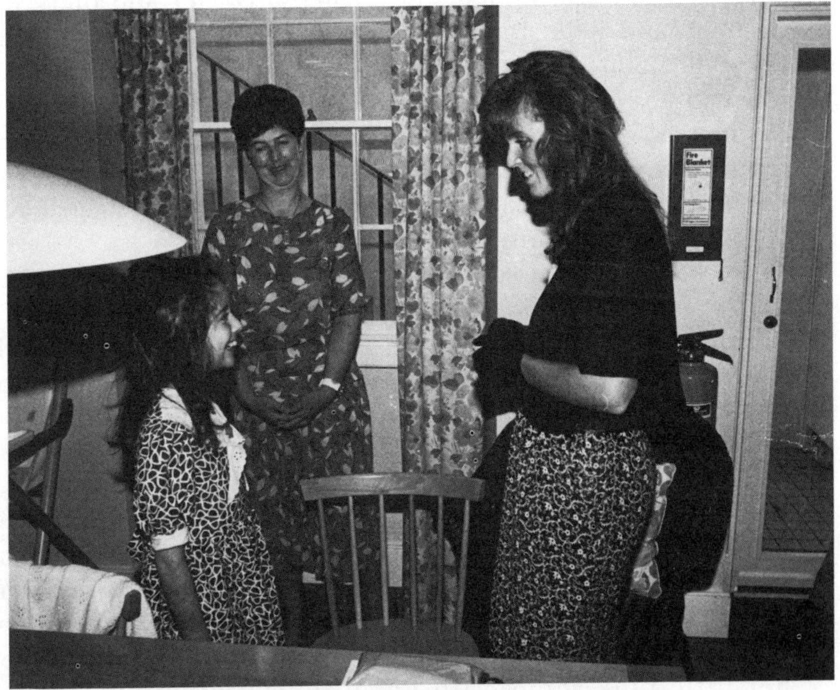

*Gillian and myself meeting The Duchess of York, at the opening of 'Home from Home' (July 1990)*

# 19. Returning Home

It is said that everyone should be famous for fifteen minutes in their lives. Gillian's fifteen minutes of fame came when we stepped off an Aer Lingus flight on the afternoon of 27th July. Gillian and myself were absolutely delighted to be returning home triumphant just six weeks after the transplant. We stepped off the plane quietly and began to walk through the corridors towards the Arrivals building. Suddenly we turned a corner and there were Brendan and Kelli. It was truly quite euphoric. Gillian ran into Brendan's outstretched arms and it was magic. We hugged each other in absolute happiness and next moment the cameras were flashing as we continued our walk together along the red carpet towards the Presidential Suite. The photographers flashed their cameras just steps ahead of us and all the other passengers looked to see who the celebrity was.

As we entered the area where my parents and our close friends were waiting, an audible gasp ensued when they caught their first glimpse of Gillian. Brendan and myself have agreed this triumphant return home for Gillian was the highlight of our whole life. It was all just sheer magic. Within the confines of the Presidential suite the champagne corks popped and everyone including Gillian, toasted her health and happiness.

We were on an emotional high for a while. Nothing mattered, Gillian had beaten all the odds. It was fantastic. Our family had survived the end stage of cystic fibrosis and Gillian now had a new pair of healthy lungs. We all said it was the closest we would ever come to a miracle. That first night home, Gillian went to sleep in her little pink room, with her little white dresser and pine wardrobe. The next morning she woke up and jumped out of bed to begin a new day without the terrible coughing fits reminiscent of her pre-transplant days. It was truly fabulous.

The day after we came home, our next door neighbour, Nuala said to me over the fence, "Veronica, I was so upset the day you went off that I couldn't see Gillian to say goodbye to her because I truly didn't think we would ever see her again. I just can't get over her, it's just great. She was so thin and sick I didn't think she would stand up to that operation. I nearly died when I heard she was on the phone to home after three days. It's amazing what they can do."

People came and went and marvelled at her appearance. Superquinn, a local supermarket sent up two huge square cakes with "Welcome Home Gillian". All Gillian's friends, Claire, Sarah, Eanna, Nicky and Karl Houtz, Eoin, Aifric, Marie and all the Doyles, were delighted she was home.

A week later we returned to R.T.E. and had another interview with Pat Kenny, who was delighted to see Gillian looking so well. Pat presented her with an enormous pink dog with long floppy ears called "Sad Sam" and said it was a present from the staff of the show.

We went off for a week's holiday in a caravan in Silver Strand, half an hour along the coast from our home. The caravan belonged to friends of ours and it was housed in a big green field on the edge of the cliff with a spectacular view of the sea. It was Gillian's long time wish to have a family holiday in a hot climate and stay in a caravan. She now at least fulfilled part of that wish. The hot climate would have to wait a while, but the weather was sunny that week and we thoroughly enjoyed ourselves. London and hospitals were forgotten, as if they had never existed. The long red scar down Gillian's chest was the only reminder of what had happened. Gillian had no problem ascending and descending the hundred steps up and down to the beach, several times each day. We played tennis outside the caravan as the sun went down each evening before driving off somewhere for our evening meal. Gillian and

Kelli would cross the field late at night, with a torch between them and only Gillian's hearty laugh would break the silence of the night. Brendan and myself would sit on two chairs outside the caravan and say, "Listen to her, isn't it great".

We found it difficult to comprehend our good fortune. Only Gillian seemed as usual to take everything in her stride. Brendan and myself were real doting parents and both kept saying, "Isn't she lovely". Kelli would give her the odd side glance as if to say, "It's really happened, you're okay".

We were just beginning to really unwind and relax when our week was over and it was time to return home. At this stage Gillian had a lovely sun tan after the weeks spent in the park in London, and re-inforced by the holiday. Between the tan and the extra weight some people didn't recognise her. One day the two girls walked down town and they met a friend of Kelli's who said, "How is Gillian?" Kelli gave one of her side glances at Gill and the child laughed and said, "Oh, I'm sorry Gillian I thought you were a Spanish student, you look great."

Everyone in Harcourt Street hospital was delighted to see Gill looking so well. No-one could get over how well she looked. They called her their V.I.P. Dr Denham checked her chest and laughed saying, "That's the clearest I've ever heard your chest Gillian." He said it was great she had remained so stable throughout the whole thing and commented on the enormous input into her. I told him it was time they got a transplant programme going here for cystics and he said, "Bit by bit."

The rest of the summer flew by and soon it was time to return to school. Gillian donned a wine tunic belonging to Kelli and cream blouse. She looked in the mirror, flicked her long dark hair back and giggled, "I really never thought I'd ever wear this uniform again."

# 20. *Living Post-Transplant*

Life settled down, and people thought we had achieved a miracle cure for Gillian. It was perceived rather like a fairy tale. However, it would be most unfair to let anyone who has a child with cystic fibrosis think a transplant is the end of all your problems.

Gillian was told to go home and enjoy a normal life. Gillian didn't know what a normal life was. She had spent a total of three months in school in her whole life. We sent her back to school last September and thought everything was going to be fine, it wasn't. Within a few weeks the problems emerged.

She would come home and say, "I can't take all those children. I feel cooped up in a cage for five hours every day."

She was overpowered by the large numbers, 38 children, in the class. The amount of work being covered was also too much for Gillian. She felt totally inadequate, she was in a class with younger children but Gill wasn't happy being with younger children. She was so advanced and mature in some ways and yet she didn't have the academic skills to go along with this level of maturity. She had been protected, and lived artificially in a cocoon-type existence for three years prior to the operation, and now we expected her to slot back without a problem. We were so caught up emotionally in the whole thing that we were completely unrealistic in our expectations for Gillian, three months after a heart and lung transplant.

On Saturday afternoon, 15th September, I phoned Monica Anglim to have a chat and see if Siobhan was well. We agreed it was a gruelling experience from which it was going to take us all a while to recover. They had spent a full three months in England initially. Although Siobhan was quite well they had been returning to London for a day or two every week. Monica and myself agreed that trying to hold down jobs, business, and a family together was a daunting task, when one had to go out of the country for a transplant. The extra expense, stress and strain, and disruption made it almost impossible to cope with. Transplantation in itself is enormous without the extra burdens.

Anyway, Monica and myself said we would have to get together and have an evening out somewhere in the near future. Her concluding comments about Siobhan were, "We have done everything possible and she will live as God wants her to."

Can you imagine the shock I felt two days later when I picked up the paper on Monday morning and staring me in the face was the following heading: "Heart/Lung Girl Dies". Siobhan Anglim had died suddenly on the Sunday.

Brendan and myself were very disillusioned by this awful news. We knew how hard Siobhan's family had fought for her. We had witnessed their anguish and anxiety the few days we were in Harefield. Like ourselves, with Gillian, they had put everything into trying to save Siobhan's life. It didn't seem right they had received so little from the transplant. Five short months and even some of that hadn't been good quality life.

Suddenly it all looked different from the initial euphoria of coming home. It was going to be more complex than we thought. So many people kept saying how marvellous it all was when they looked at Gillian, who looked a picture of health. I knew it was great, the proof was in front of me but I didn't feel it. I looked at Gillian one evening running around playing on the road and it suddenly all hit me.

"This is what most people have and expect for their children. Why did we have to go through all we have gone through to get this for our child? Children are supposed to be able to run around, play and do things and look forward to the future."

For the first time since Gillian was diagnosed, I resented cystic fibrosis and what it had done to our lives. The price of everything just seemed to have been very high.

Gillian still had to go into Harcourt Street Hospital once a week, to have blood taken to monitor her body functions, especially the Cyclosporin levels, which control rejection. Her veins were so bad from all the needles over the summer that it was difficult to get a good vein at times. She also had to return to London for several days every month. This involved loss of business or salary and more haggling with the Health Board. It was all money.

We would be just back when it was time to go off again. Each time we returned to London she would have a lung biopsy, which meant she had a general anaesthetic. I re-lived the transplant every time they took her off to put her asleep. Then we would have to wait twenty-four hours for the results of the biopsy.

In October, Gillian developed shingles and wound up in Harcourt Street in isolation, on a drip receiving massive doses of acyclovir, an anti-viral drug. It seemed as if nothing had changed. She had spent Hallowe'en in hospital for as long as she could remember. She had been in hospital for three days and it was the day before Hallowe'en. Gillian told Dr Denham she wanted to go home because she had arrangements made for Hallowe'en, and could she continue with oral acyclovir for the rest of the treatment. He let her out and off she went to a party and bonfire the next evening.

I worried it was too soon to be out and about but Gillian wouldn't listen. She wanted to live to capacity with her new found lease of life. She looked at me and said, "Mum, will you please stop worrying about me or you will spoil the whole thing, and that's not what we went through it all for. Please relax and let me be. I'll be alright because I really believe in it, that it can work for me and it will." She kissed me and ran off. Maybe she was right.

I needed to calm down emotionally and re-assess our lives. Whenever I felt very tired, things always looked worse. I had returned to school a week after Gillian's first trip back to London and just one month after the triumphant return at the end of July. People kept saying, "What do you do with all your spare time, now you don't have physiotherapy to do for hours every day?" I would reply, "I don't do anything and I don't seem to have any spare time. The miracle is how we managed to keep going at the pace we did for so long."

I seemed to be doing everything at a much slower pace. Una told me I was looking for too much too soon. "You want everything just to slot in as if the last ten years have never happened. You will have to give yourself time to re-adjust and accept the reality of your new situation and what it involves." She also said she saw an aggression in me that was never there before. This surprised me and I had a good think about what she had said.

It seemed as if Gillian was the only one things were very good for during those first few months after we came home. Brendan was very quiet and rested a lot. He would sometimes say, "Ron, it all took a lot more out of us than we thought." He would mention the weeks when he came back home, leaving Gill in intensive care, and trying to work while, at any minute, thinking the phone could ring with bad news.

We often discussed the reason it had taken so much out of us. There were many factors we decided. Some obvious, as it had been an enormous undertaking. But if we could have had the transplant in Dublin and could have stayed together throughout and had no worries about going back and forth, it would have been a lot easier.

Brendan said, "Just look at the file of letters between yourself and the Health Board over the last few years, not to mention phone calls, and you'll know why it took so much out of you."

It all came down to finance. We decided that if we had been wealthy enough not to have had to bother looking for money from our Health Board, half of the stress, strain and anxiety would have been eliminated. It was the one regret I ever had to bother with them. Other people we spoke to in Great Ormond Street agreed that there was enough stress going through the ordeal of a transplant without added worry and hassle over money.

One person told me the child's Attendance Allowance had been stopped as soon as her daughter had the transplant. No-one seemed to understand that the level of care needed after a transplant is as high, if not higher than before if the patient is to do well.

The Cystic Fibrosis Organisation in England recognized that it was an expensive time and I believe U.K. residents are given up to £500 to help with extra expenses.

It was amazing, we had learnt so much about people through our experience. We received support from the most unusual quarters and this helped retain our faith in humanity. We had never been into money much before this experience. It was never that important. In future it will be more important to us.

However, over the Christmas holidays we had a good rest and began to reap the benefits of our new found quality of life. Gillian was getting stronger by the day. She was now learning the flute. It was just great to listen to her playing "Jingle Bells".

I was beginning to unwind emotionally and once again feel all the good things that had happened for Gillian. I forced myself to stop thinking and dwelling on the past and how difficult it had all been. Gillian herself had helped me to stop worrying about the ever present threat of rejection. She was very right, worrying would "spoil everything".

I came to terms with everything around Christmas and remembered my promise the night before the transplant, that I would accept "his will" afterwards.

Young Orla Roche went onto the active list in November but she deteriorated very rapidly which is often the case with cystic fibrosis. Sadly, Orla died shortly after Christmas, without ever getting the chance Gillian had received. Una, her Mum, phoned me the evening after she died and said, "Veronica, we weren't as lucky as you, but the hope of it helped us to live through the final weeks and I'm glad we tried."

It was our best Christmas in ten years, simply because Gillian was not coughing continuously, and gone were the endless hours of physiotherapy. We were all at home together for nine days and we relaxed as a family together, without the interruptions of the rigorous, disciplined routine the cystic fibrosis treatment involved every few hours. To just wake up and have breakfast without saying, "Wait until Gillian has had her nebulizer and therapy" was just lovely. The nicest part was late at night, to be able to go off to bed without going through the ritual again, having done it already twice during the day. No matter how late it was, the nebulizer and therapy could not be missed even once.

The once or twice we ever said, "Just this once, we'll skip the third therapy", two or three hours later Gillian would be coughing and unable to breathe and it would have to be done in the middle of the night. So anyone with healthy children will not be able to understand me saying, this Christmas was so special because all this treatment was gone and Gillian was able to breathe freely and do everything a ten-year-old does. I once again began to feel it really was great, as well as just knowing it.

We finally knew how special and lucky we were, because most cystic families never experience what we were experiencing. They experience not having to go through the ordeal of the treatment any more but only because they have lost their children.

We had rid ourselves of the shackles of the respiratory part of cystic fibrosis and subsequently a new life had been given to our child. She was really living now at ten, for the first time, as others understand living. Through the terrific input of medical science and the generosity of the donor family, at a time of great personal grief, the miracle of Gillian's success story came about.

As you have seen from the previous pages of this book it didn't just happen. It was a long hard, difficult road. The term "nothing worthwhile in life is easy" was certainly true in our case.

Gillian had made Irish medical history by becoming the first cystic fibrosis sufferer in the Republic to receive a heart and lung transplant. We were never offered a transplant by anyone, at any stage. I asked, enquired, sought, pursued, fought for, waited, hoped and finally achieved this great gift of a potential future for Gillian. The price was high for our family, financially, emotionally, physically, mentally and psychologically.

When one goes looking for a transplant, or is offered a place on a transplant waiting list, there are certain things to be borne in mind.

You are given no guarantee you will ever get a transplant.

You may have a very long traumatic wait and almost make it, only to have it cancelled. This can happen even more than once.

If you are lucky enough to get to the table, you may not get through the operation.

If you survive the transplant, you are given no guarantee of how long you will live.

There are degrees of success and hence the quality of life will depend on the level of success your transplant achieves.

If you are living in the Republic of Ireland, you will have to go to England or elsewhere for the transplant.

No-one is going to pay everything for you and it will not even be understood how expensive it all is.

After the initial six to eight weeks post transplant, you may have to return to the hospital every month for the first year or so.

Usually there will be weekly visits to your local hospital to have blood taken. Everything is very well explained at the assessment, but you only listen to the part "prolong life".

This is the reality of transplantation and I would imagine for various reasons the whole process would not suit everyone. No-one should feel any guilt by not deciding to go this route to cope with the illness of a child. I could quite understand people not even admitting to themselves they couldn't go through it, and would perhaps just not choose to recognise how ill their chid is. Or saying, "I wouldn't put him or her through it," when in fact what they really mean is they wouldn't put themselves and their family through it. It is all very personal what lengths people will go to, to hang onto life.

Regarding cystic fibrosis and transplants, it must be remembered the cystic families have usually already been through a long difficult time coping with a terrible illness affecting the daily lives of the whole family. So, when they embark on the first assessment they are usually very tired and worn out people. On the positive side, they are used to hospitals and all that goes with daily contact in a hospital environment. Cystic children, from what I have seen, are usually very determined, strong willed, vibrant people with a strong will to live. Carolyn is now waiting almost three long years and is in hospital all the time. But Gwen says Gillian has given them hope because when she met Gillian she didn't think she would make it. We pray daily that Carolyn will get the same chance Gillan got because the Mullen family truly deserve that chance.

I remember Mr John Wallwork, the surgeon in Papworth, one of the pioneers of transplants for cystics, being asked on the Wogan show how they decided who to give the transplant to with such limited resources. He replied, "We pick people who want to live! Now there is a difference between a person not wanting to die and one wanting to "live".

From this point of view Gillian was an ideal candidate. She loves life and people, each day has always been a new challenge to her.

For us it was the right decision to go looking for a transplant to prolong Gillian's life and we would do it all over again for Gillian. I once said, if only she could have three months of normal life without the awful suffering and coughing. Well, to date Gillian has had over a year of excellent living.

It has been the most exciting and worthwhile year of our lives, to witness the joy her new lease of life has brought her. She walks all over town with her friends and recently climbed Bray Head, which is 800 feet above sea level. Her loud laugh can be heard above all the other children as she runs in play.

There is a certain wildness in her whole approach to living. I'm not worried about the pink bike not being used any more, but whether Gillian gets killed, the way she goes flying all over the place on it. She talks of trading it for a bigger, stronger mountain bike. She even talks of driving a red sports car. Recently she confided to Kelli, "Kel, they don't know how long these transplants last, so I'm going to live every day as if it's my last!".

Hopefully she will have many years such as this past one to live and enjoy.

During a recent visit to Dr Denham's clinic in Harcourt Street, I was getting into the heart of something with him regarding lung function and he turned to Gillian and said, "Gillian, your Mum is still reaching for the stars."

# 21. The Future

Gillian's future is rather more uncertain than most people's. She must daily fight off, on the one hand infection because her immune system is suppressed, and on the other hand, rejection of the organs she was not born with. This is being controlled daily with anti-rejection drugs. While these two factors remain in her favour, she will continue to enjoy the marvellous quality of life she has enjoyed now for one year.

A major turning point for transplantation came in the early 1980's with the development of a revolutionary wonder anti-rejection drug called Cyclosporin, which is largely the cause of the improved longer term success rate of all transplants. Cyclosporin was developed following the discovery of an unusual fungus, dug up by a scientist in Hardanger, Norway in 1970. The drug developed from this fungus contains an amino acid yet to be found in any other life form. The drug was approved by the Food and Drug Administration in September 1983 and marketed under the name of Sandimine.

While Cyclosporin has greatly improved the prognosis for transplant patients, it is not the final solution for longterm survival because there can be toxic side effects from this drug which can effect other organs in the body. This is why the correct level of Cyclosporin in the blood stream is very important.

For Gillian, it poses more problems than non-cystic transplant patients. Although Gillian has a new heart and lungs free of cystic fibrosis, she still has a cystic body and her digestive system is still affected and hence she doesn't always absorb at the same rate all the time.

This has been a problem for her this last year, the Cyclosporin levels have fluctuated quite a lot and so they have to be monitored weekly by blood tests. If the level of cyclosporin is too low she can reject, and if they go up and remain too high they can cause damage to the liver and kidneys. Hence the weekly visits to Harcourt Street Hospital for blood tests, and constantly re-adjusting the daily amount of Cyclosporin.

Cyclosporin is the best drug to date to help transplant patients not reject their new organs, but it suppresses their whole immune system, not just the part of the new organs. If something could be developed to trick just the appropriate specific part of the immune system then transplants would advance even further.

Gillian's long term survival could be helped by advancement in management of cystic fibrosis, which she still has, and any new development which may come in the area of immunosuppression.

However, in the meantime Jo Hatton, who doesn't have cystic fibrosis and Julie Bennett, one of the first cystic fibrosis transplants in Papworth, almost six years ago, are still alive and enjoying good quality of life and this is very encouraging.

We will continue to "reach for the stars" in the daily on-going battle for Gillian's life, for the little girl who always had a talent for making a situation look normal even when it was not, and in so doing not trouble anyone. Only ourselves ever saw her moments of fatigue and suffering. Rarely did anyone else ever see the hidden pain behind her lovely smile. She bore her illness bravely with fantastic courage.

Gillian was hospitalised a total of twenty-eight times before her transplant, each time for two weeks to three months. Spending around five hundred days in Harcourt Street Children's Hospital, with needles in her arms, tubes down her nose, and hours of pounding on her lungs every day.

She took it all in her stride and accepted it all as she is taking her new lease of life, in the same matter of fact way. I think she truly deserves every minute of her new found happiness.

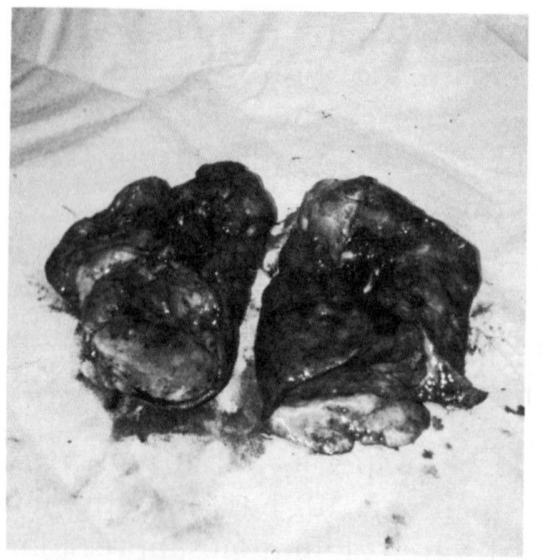

*These were the lungs with which Gillian survived for so long!*

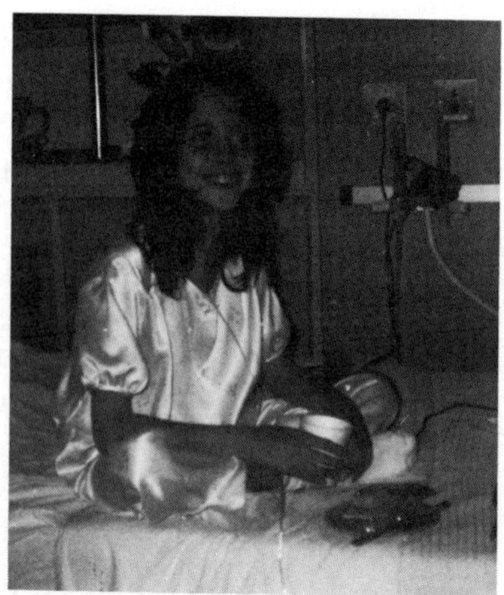

*Three days post-operation*

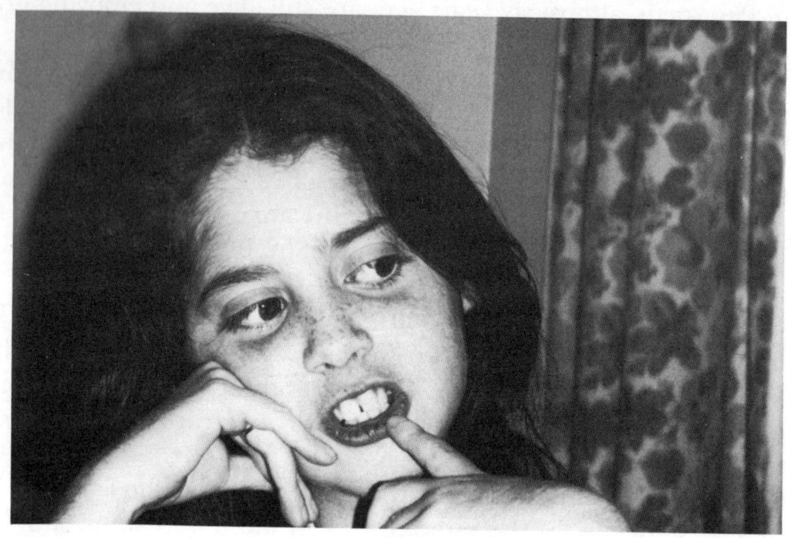

*Gillian as she is now.*

# *Appendix*

"Cystic fibrosis is, without any doubt, the worst illness to afflict children. It has a cure rate of 0%. A childhood cancer carries a cure rate of 50% or greater. It is a disease which inflicts great suffering on the child and the family, in contrast to other diseases such as muscular dystrophy, which although fatal, do not cause any suffering. Where a child does die from cystic fibrosis, the mode of death is virtually akin to slow suffocation and is the most miserable sight I am ever likely to witness. Speaking as someone who had lost his own child, I can confidently say that there are many things worse than being dead, and that terminal cystic fibrosis is indeed one of those things."

These are the words of Dr Brian Denham who looked after Gillian for six years in Harcourt Street Hospital, and worked so hard to keep her alive when others gave up. He also says, "We are all waiting for the cure for cystic fibrosis. Heart/lung transplant does not cure the disease, substitutes transplant disease, which as you know, is fairly terrible in itself for the even worse disease of cystic fibrosis. The Cystic Fibrosis Association has spent enormous amounts of money in research over the years and this has resulted in a gradual improvement in the quality of lifestyle of all children with cystic fibrosis, rather in the way that the motor car has developed, a slow but steady improvement. The cure, if it ever comes, will be like the development of rocket power. It will occur suddenly, perhaps very unexpectedly and it may or may not occur in my lifetime. There are several promising avenues of research into a cure, but in addition, there is a great deal of research going on into improving the quality of life, which present patients have, and many doctors and research personnel are devoting their entire lives to this.

"I would also remark that the care of children with cystic fibrosis requires an exceptional level of dedication from the parents, and also from all the medical and nursing personnel involved. The amount of work which has to be put into caring for three or four children with cystic fibrosis, is the same as needs to be put into caring for three or four hundred normal children, and of course none of them are private patients, so that the icing which would be on the cake in terms of disposable income, both to the hospital and the medical personnel concerned, in the case of normal patients, is removed and this is one of the things which makes it difficult to enlist really high calibre people into cystic fibrosis care."

There is only one thing I cannot agree with, in our case anyway. So far the difference between a cystic fibrosis patient and a transplant patient is much greater than Dr Denham seems to think. I know we have been very lucky and Gillian is a "good transplant patient", but once the initial trauma of the whole thing has subsided, the gap between the two ways of life cannot be compared. There are enormous differences. It is like living with two different children.

On the subject of a cure, a recent article in the *London Telegraph* sounded exciting.

***Gene Therapy Breakthrough***

Dorothy Clyde explains the potential treatment for a major disease.

Cystic fibrosis is the most prevalent life-threatening, inherited disease in the United Kingdom. Now advances in genetics are paving the way for a dramatic treatment through gene transplants. Progressive lung disease is the most insidious complication that sufferers contend with, it is the prime cause of premature death.

At present, heart-lung transplant operations can be performed on patients with very severe symptoms. This, however, is an extreme form of treatment, available to only a small proportion of cystic fibrosis sufferers. This is partly due to the shortage of suitable donors.

In August 1989, a revolutionary discovery accelerated the pace of research in the field. A team of three North American scientists – Lap Chee Tsui, Francis Collins and Jack Riordan – succeeded in isolating the defective cystic fibrosis gene. It was the first step towards treatment by replacing the faulty gene with a normal alternative.

In September 1990, Collins, with his partner James Wilson, successfully performed such an efficacious exchange on pancreatic cells in a test tube. Following this important breakthrough, research is continuing in an attempt to find a technique to replace faulty genes inside the living human body.

Viruses are being considered as potentially suitable vehicles for the transfer of healthy genes to cells in the body. An important characteristic of viruses is their ability to invade cells and implant genetic material without difficulty.

By means of genetic engineering, the normal gene (necessary to replace the defective cystic fibrosis gene) can be added to a virus's own genetic material. Within the cell, this genetically engineered virus can implant the normal gene into defective cells; this change overrides the effect of the flawed gene, thus correcting the host cell.

There are problems to overcome, however. Many viruses are disease-inducing; some viruses are feared to be carcinogenic. Caution, therefore, must be exercised so as to ensure that the "transfer virus" has no adverse side effects.

How best to introduce the virus into the body is also problematic. At present, the most promising technique for delivering the virus, and thus healthy genes, is by aerosol. The viruses are inhaled, thus directly reaching the lungs; there they are assimilated into the cells, bringing with them the normal gene to replace the defective cystic fibrosis gene in the lung cells.

Such a development would introduce a significant degree of new freedom into the lives of cystic fibrosis sufferers; their reliance on demanding treatments could be minimised. Most importantly, their lives could be considerably extended.

We all hope these things will come about soon, as it is obviously the solution for cystic sufferers rather than heart/lung transplants. However, in the meantime, children and young adults like Gillian, who have run out of time will continue to depend on the marvellous work being carried out in the field of transplantation in the United Kingdom.

Here in Ireland there is an excellent heart transplant programme in operation and it really is time for a heart/lung programme.

Dr Denham called for this in the *Irish Medical Times* on the 18 May 1990. He said, "The annual demand for CF patients, should a programme be set up in this country, would be between seven and fifteen a year.

"To date fifteen Irish patients have been assessed abroad for possible transplants. But so far no Irish CF patient has been transplanted."

He believes it would make economic sense to have an assessment unit in Ireland and fund transplants here rather than the Health Boards paying for patients to be assessed and treated abroad.

An assessment can cost between £3,000 and £5,000 and must be repeated once or twice a year on patients awaiting transplants. Some of the fifteen patients have been assessed on a number of occasions in England. The cost of a heart/lung transplant is estimated at £150,000. The CF patient's heart can later be transplanted into another recipient.

A heart/lung transplant is the only option for some terminal patients with cystic fibrosis, but only a relatively small number out of the total CF population would be suitable for this procedure.

There are 34 patients in Ireland, out of the total CF population of about 700, in whom heart/lung transplants would be considered as an option, though it is believed not all would be suitable.

While the expertise is already available in Ireland, funding and back-up facilities would be needed. A survey by the Medical and Scientific Advisory Committee of the need for heart/lung transplants has just been completed. It indicates that the Department of Health needs to examine whether patients should be still referred overseas or whether the service should be provided here, according to its secretary, Dr Denham.

The following information was supplied to me by Mike Rigglesford from the public relations department of the U.K. Transplant Service.

Last year, 1990 – 348 heart transplants and 94 heart/lung transplants were carried out in the U.K. Of the heart/lung transplants 48 were domino, which means the cystic hearts were re-used.

At the present time there are 258 patients on the waiting list for heart transplants and 230 people waiting for a heart/lung transplant.

These operations are now being carried out in about ten centres in the U.K.

It is six years now since the heart/lung programme started in the U.K., and Ireland should surely have at least one centre by now!

The survival rates from statistics available are: up to one year 74% heart and 62% heart/lungs; up to four years 67% heart and 43% heart/lungs.

I said to Mike, "So the greatest loss is in the first year." His reply, "Sweetheart, if they can survive the first few months, they have a good chance. Please tell people, not only to carry a donor card, but they must make their wishes known to their relatives."

Suitable donor organs never became available for Carolyn. Sadly, after waiting and hoping for almost three years, Carolyn lost her battle for life on 22 September 1991.